# TO BE POPULAR OR SMART: THE BLACK PEER GROUP

## by Jawanza Kunjufu

African American Images

Chicago, Illinois

Cover Illustration by Yaounde Olu
Photo Credits, William Hall


First Edition
Second Printing


Copyright © 1988 by Jawanza Kunjufu

# TABLE OF CONTENTS

Introduction . . . . . . . . . . . . . . . . . . . . . . . . . . . . . . . . . . . . v

Chapter One — Student Profiles . . . . . . . . . . . . . . . . . . . . . 1

Chapter Two — The Psychology of Being Black . . . . . . . 11

Chapter Three — Students: Confront the Fear . . . . . . . . 33

Chapter Four — Parents . . . . . . . . . . . . . . . . . . . . . . . . . . . 51

Chapter Five — Teachers . . . . . . . . . . . . . . . . . . . . . . . . . . 67

Chapter Six — Community . . . . . . . . . . . . . . . . . . . . . . . . . 85

Conclusion . . . . . . . . . . . . . . . . . . . . . . . . . . . . . . . . . . . . 95

Footnotes . . . . . . . . . . . . . . . . . . . . . . . . . . . . . . . . . . . . . 98

# INTRODUCTION

I am a Christian, my Lord and Savior is Jesus Christ. I want everyone to know, because some people assume if you have an African name, believe in self-determination, don't eat meat, and believe in God, you must be from another religious persuasion. All of my books, *Countering the Conspiracy to Destroy Black Boys, Volumes I-II*; *Developing Positive Self-Images and Discipline in Black Children*; *Motivating Black Youth to Work*; and *Lessons from History: A Celebration in Blackness, Elementary and High School Editions*; were inspired by God.

I do not consider myself a writer. I believe that writers enjoy what they do, perform it regularly, and many write every day. They have told me their best work was never released to the public. Writing has an opposite motivation for me; I do not enjoy writing, I don't write regularly, and I write mainly to present my views to the public. I have been obedient to God in my writing. I am very sensitive and perceptive and have observed the problems of Black boys, the difficulties in securing self-esteem for Black youth, their lack of motivation, and their embarrassment in learning "Negro" history only in February. I had planned to write a book about the drug problem in our community or about economic development, but the Lord had other ideas.

Let me paint the picture of how the Lord works. It was February 25, 1988 in Philadelphia. The program was for Catholic and public school educators. I had spoken for five hours about how to improve academic achievement for African-American children. The workshop was concluding when God used a parent named Namorah to inspire *To be Popular or Smart: The Black Peer Group*. I had previously stated in the workshop that four of the major factors contributing to this academic gap were: low teacher expectations, poor parent support, low student self-esteem, and an irrelevant curriculum taught with an inappropriate methodology for many African-American students. The last factor was the peer group. I said, "It is very possible for parents to be supportive and teachers to have high expectations, and it all go for naught because the Black peer group is more concerned about what clothes you wear, how well you dance or play basketball, than academic achievement."

What did I say that for! Namorah testified about her son, who was a very good student and was attending an excellent high school, but was being negatively influenced by his peer group. Other educators became parents, and they spilled their tears for the next two hours about this "silent killer" destroying African-American youth from striving toward academic achievement.

The Lord was just as clear with this book as He was with the others. "You will write what I want you to write. I have not inspired you (yet) to write a book about drugs or economics. At this time, I want you to write about the peer group, its impact on academic achievement." Because I am not a writer, but I am obedient (in this area), I know the only books I write that will be successful will be those inspired by God.

After educators testified as parents about the marked decline of their offspring as peer pressure increased, they reverted back to teachers and described their frustration in the classroom trying to motivate youth with thirty to one odds. In most classrooms, you have one person promoting academics, the teacher, and thirty students promoting talking, playing, and clowning. We must find strategies to improve those odds, to give teachers a better chance of winning and to avoid teacher burnout.

The phenomenon of peer pressure and its impact on academic achievement has reached catastrophic proportions. It has now reached a point that to do well academically in school is to act white and risk being called a nerd or a brainiac. For males, the peer pressure is so great, you may be called a sissy. Can you imagine the ancestor's children, who built the first civilization and taught the ancient Greek scholars, attributing academic achievement to being White? Please do not discern this solely to integration. There are schools that only African-American students attend, there are *no* White students, and they still say to be smart is to be white.

Our students go to many kinds of schools. Some attend all-Black schools in low-income neighborhoods, others attend all-Black schools in middle-income communities, others attend integrated, elite, magnet high schools where admission is based on a test, some attend integrated schools in the suburbs, and lastly some attend coed, homogeneous, private schools. This book is written for students in all five circumstances. In Philadelphia, the audience described experiences from all five settings. They were surprised that in the latter three environments—magnet schools, integrated suburban schools, and private schools—negative peer pressure still existed for their children. Many parents worked very hard to live in more affluent neighborhoods and pay tuition so their children could be "inspired" by a positive peer group. Other parents like Namorah or my wife and I were able to have our children admitted into elite magnet schools, only to find this silent killer there too.

The book is divided into six chapters. The first chapter ("Student Profiles") contains vignettes of what our students experience in their own words. The second chapter ("The Psychology of Being Black") describes from a historical perspective, the impact slavery and the present caste system in America have had on academic motivation. Chapter Three ("Students: Confront the Fear") attempts to get students to dig within themselves and psychoanalyze their thoughts and actions. Chapter Four ("Parents") encourages parents to network with other parents experiencing similar circumstances, and how they can deprogram their children from this silent killer. Chapter Five ("Teachers") provides strategies on how teachers can improve the 30:1 odds, and give greater credence to academic achievement over athletics. The last chapter ("Community") challenges the community to motivate our youth by providing human and financial resources that create a vision to inspire our youth to excellence.

The big debate in America is recognizing the racial disparity in income levels, educational attainment, life expectancy, health care, adequate housing, etc. Whose responsibility is it to close the gap reported every twenty years by a "blue ribbon" committee? The two extreme positions are either the government or the victim. The media, owned by people that created the disparity, give more time to those advocates that place the burden squarely on the victim. People like the late Clarence Pendleton and the economist Thomas Sowell, are given all the air time they want to erroneously compare immigrants to slaves. Harold Cruse and Eleanor Holmes Norton are given very little time to describe a more balanced approach. It's ironic that Louis Farrakhan who also advocates, as does Thomas Sowell, placing the burden on the victim and doing away with welfare, is given very little coverage of his self-determination philosophy. This may be because Farrakhan, like most nationalists, recognizes that before we provide our solutions, let's be clear about how we got in this mess and who put us here, so that when we recreate a better world, we won't use the same value system of the oppressor with people who have a darker hue. Oppression is oppression whether it's administered by a European or Duvalier, Amin or some "Negro" mayor in the United States.

This book will look at one of the internal "silent killers"—peer pressure—and its impact on academic achievement. I in no way am advocating that if the peer group had a positive mental attitude, it could eradicate all the external factors (racism—overt and institutional—monopoly capitalism, sexism, etc.) that created most of our problems. We must demand excellence of ourselves and agitate and advocate justice from the larger society.

This book is not concerned with the students who are exceptions to the rule. Those students are not affected by peer pressure, often are very individualistic, and while doing well academically, have no commitment to the race. I wish them well and will expect to see them return to the Black community, when their dream of becoming chief executive officer of a Fortune 500 company does not materialize. In the meantime, let's listen to the majority of students, who speak in Chapter One, as they describe their experiences—to be popular or smart.

*Many of our youth would rather be popular and cool than smart.*

# STUDENT PROFILES

Kareem Abdul-Jabbar paints the picture with these words:

> I got there [Holy Providence School in Cornwall Heights, right outside of Philadelphia] and immediately found I could read better than anyone in the school. My father's example and my mother's training had made that come easy; I could pick up a book, read it out loud, pronounce the words with proper inflections and actually know what they meant. When the nuns found this out they paid a lot of attention, once even asking me, a fourth grader, to read to the seventh grade. When the kids found this out I became a target. . . .
>
> It was my first time away from home, my first experience in an all-black situation, and I found myself being punished for doing everything I'd ever been taught was right. I got all A's and was hated for it; I spoke correctly and was called a punk. I had to learn a new language simply to be able to deal with the threats. I had good manners and was a good little boy and paid for it with my hide.[1]

I will look at ten students from the five different types of high schools. There will be six lower-achieving students and four higher-achieving students. The profiles will include six male students and four female students. These numbers were chosen for a reason. Peer pressure has had a negative impact on academic achievement; therefore, while we want to show in four vignettes how students were able to weather the storm, we want more attention given to the many pitfalls. I also wanted a slightly greater male population because they are more influenced by their peer group, which may be because males see fewer positive adult male role models than females do. The stories told below are real, only the names have been changed.

## Lower-achieving female students

*Kathy*

Kathy is a sophomore at Academy of Our Lady, a Catholic school for girls. The school has a 100 percent Black student body and an evenly balanced integrated staff. Her parents have worked hard to send their four children to private schools, with Kathy being the last. Her older siblings are excellent role models; one is a lawyer, one is in grad school, and the other is a junior in college. Kathy scored well on the Iowa Test in elementary school, with a composite of 8 stanine (only twenty percent nationwide had higher scores) and a year above her grade level in reading and math. This is what Kathy had to say about her school experience.

"It was my freshman year, and I heard people calling me stuck up. Some of the same people calling me that also wore designer clothes and Louis Vitton bags. (We normally wore uniforms except on special occasions.) I couldn't understand why they were talking about me and dressing the same way until we got back our midterm test scores in English. I received the highest score with a 97 and my teacher based her curve off my grade. Three students received 91 but they got a B. One of them had been calling me stuck up and now she said I thought I was better than them. Hey, I don't need the hassle so now I wear cheap earrings and leave my Louis Vitton bag at home, sit in the back of the class, and don't make no waves. I still do okay, they don't talk about me and I still got a 76 on the final exam. I mean, it's passing."

## Aisha

Aisha attends Chicago Vocational High School, better known as CVS. It has a very large student body located in one of the most affluent neighborhoods in the Black community. Student achievement is mediocre with approximately twenty-five percent of the students scoring at the national average. Aisha is an average student, she had a composite of 4 on the Iowa Test and a C average on her report card. Her parents are no longer together, but the father spends a lot of time with his daughter. He told me teachers have always told him Aisha has the potential if she will apply herself. Aisha is a junior. Let's listen to Aisha describe her experiences.

"I don't like school. I don't see how it relates to the real world. I'm going to get my diploma and get me a job typing at some bank. On Friday, I'm going to buy as many dresses as I can with my check. I guess that's why I cut class. All I need is the diploma. That's why I don't take hard subjects in math and science, because I don't want to mess up my grade point average. I've seen those nerds that study all the time. I have relatives like them, but they still end up working the same kind of places I want to work. Hey, I don't want to be no nerd, plus I'm not doing no more than what's required."

## Lower Achieving Male Students

### Lemont

Lemont goes to Whitney Young Magnet High School. Lemont wants to be an electrical engineer. He has natural ability, scoring at the 8 to 9 stanines on the Iowa and high school citywide exams. Lemont will be a junior in the fall. In elementary school he was a B student, doing primarily what was required. His mother tries to monitor his recreational time and supplements his school work with additional materials. Young High School is a magnet school, requiring a test for admittance. The year Lemont was admitted, 5,000 people applied but only 500 were admitted. Parents feel very confident that a child attending this school will benefit from teachers with high expectations and a positive peer group. The school is predominately Black and Hispanic with a 25% White population. Lemont describes his experiences.

"I can get an A on any test I want. It doesn't matter whether it's biology, algebra, English, history, drafting or gym. In some of my classes, there have been five tests and I've gotten five different grades, A, B, C, D, F. It's hard being serious the entire year, I've got too many distractions—the fellas, the women, sports, and my music. I could be in honors classes, but I don't want my partners to tease me and call me a fag. I usually sit in the back of the class and clown, and sometimes I don't go to class at all. I'm tight with my friends and the women love me. I don't see the guys respecting the nerds or the women chasing after them. I would like to get A's or B's, it would really get my parents off my back, but I can't be serious for forty straight weeks, plus I'd rather be down with my partners."

### Darryl

Darryl goes to Du Sable High School, one of the poorest schools in the city. It is known for many things, ranging from the school that Harold Washington, John Johnson and Dempsey Travis graduated from, to now being a school with one of the highest dropout and pregnancy rates in the country. Darryl lives across the street from the school, in the Robert Taylor Homes. His mother is a devout Christian and has instilled these values into Darryl. He tried hard to avoid the gangs to and from school. He was an A student in elementary school but did not score high enough to attend one of the elite magnet schools. Darryl describes his experiences.

"I remember in my freshman English class we had to write an essay about whatever we wanted. I wrote about how I wanted Jesus to remove the gangs from the projects. My White teacher asked me what magazine I copied from. She said it was an outstanding essay, but she did not believe that I wrote it. I guess that's what did it, she thought Black people could not write that well about what they truly felt. I started sitting in the back of the class and clowning with my friends. I'm even thinking about joining a gang."

### Michael

Michael attends a private Catholic school named Leo. It is an all-male school with a 100 percent Black student population and nearly that percentage for staff. It is an older school whose demographics have changed with the neighborhood. Michael is an only child from working class parents. They really can't afford tuition, but they value education and so they have adjusted their expenses to insure that Michael goes to a good school. Michael is a "bookworm"; he voluntarily goes to the library, he won his elementary school spelling bee, and he received honorable mention on his science fair project. Michael describes his experiences.

"I just couldn't take it. First they called me four eyes, then a brainiac, they picked me last in gym, and some bullies said they would kick my a____ if I didn't do their homework and give them the answers for the test. Nobody seems to understand. My teachers always call on me to do something or answer the question. My friends get upset about this and take it out on me. My parents say to ignore my friends, but I keep trying to tell them at 14, you cannot ignore your friends. I'm not doing as well in school as I should, I'm distracted and I resent giving people answers. I've noticed people that are not doing well in school don't have these problems. It's made me sort of lay back so I can be like everybody else."

### Doug

Doug attends Evanston Township High School, a school

that prides itself on being very liberal on racial balance and equity issues. The school is very large and is proud of its broad curriculum, especially toward college preparation. It resides in the same city with the prestigious Northwestern University. Doug is the oldest of five brothers. He is expected to continue the legacy of college graduates. The two previous generations both attended college and they strongly inspire Doug to follow in their footsteps. Doug is an average student with scores in the 5 stanines, but he had all A's in elementary school because he studied hard. His parents commend their son for studying beyond their own high expectations. Doug describes his experiences.

"I noticed during my first week that African-American students hung out in the back of the school and European-American students stood in the front. I observed a similar separation in the lunchroom. The problem I had was that most of the students in my classes who were serious were Caucasian students. I wanted to study with them and a few times I hung out with them in the library or in study hall. I was afraid of doing this in the lunchroom or after school. One time, Joey a European-American student invited me to the museum with his family. My partners that I walk home with kept riding me and calling me an oreo. Sometimes, I get tired of being in two worlds. I know my grades would improve if I studied and shared notes with Caucasian students, but I live with African-Americans. I guess you could say I value more my partners than my grades."

## Higher achieving females

*Kisha*

Kisha attends Du Sable, previously described as a school in the heart of the low-income African-American community. Kisha has been a very good student all of her life. She has scored in 7 stanines on the Iowa Basic Skills Test, and she scored 21 on the ACT. She was a finalist in the National

Achievement contest. Her father, a single parent, is very proud of his daughter. Kisha describes her experiences.

"I am very strong willed, I guess that also makes me a loner. People wanted me to go to a better school, but I said I can do well right here, close to home. My teachers are very proud of me, but they always tell me I'm different from everybody else. Sometimes, they have said these things in front of my friends. It has not made that relationship any easier. I have to fight a lot, it was worse when I was a freshman, but now my graduating class has shrunk from 900 students down to 254. I think what saved me is my strong will, fighting ability, and because I'm a girl. I don't think a boy could be a loner at Du Sable, have good grades, and score 21 on the ACT."

*Donna*

Donna attends Evanston Township, the suburban high school near Northwestern University. Donna has two brothers and one sister. Her mother is a teacher and her father works at the post office in Chicago. They moved across the Chicago border so their children could go to better schools. Donna has been on the honor roll the first two years. The following school year, she attended advanced placement classes. Donna describes her experiences.

"I don't understand this black stuff. I'm the only African-American student in the oratorical contest being conducted in the auditorium after school, and African-American students didn't even come to show their support. You would think they would be proud of me, but instead they call me white. I'm not white, look at me, do I look white? I'm sick of this black-white stuff, I just want to be me. I'm not stuck up, but they said I am because I don't listen to the same radio station they listen to. I like listening to all kinds of music, rap, rock, jazz, classical, reggae, you name it. I'll be glad when I graduate, maybe I can go to a college where what you do won't be confined to your race."

## Higher achieving male students

*Kofi*

Kofi attends Leo High School, previously described as the private school for males. Kofi has three younger sisters all being raised by his mother. She is very much aware of the conspiracy to destroy Black boys and feels a private male school would teach Kofi to be disciplined. Kofi wants to be a doctor and has always done well in science fairs. His test scores are in the 8 stanines in math and science and 5 in language arts. Kofi will be a sophomore in the fall. Kofi describes his experiences.

"I wish I went to a school where everybody was serious about school, including the teachers. Sometimes, the teachers spend more time disciplining and administering than they do teaching. My freshman year was a rough one, you leave a real small elementary school and go to a large high school where everybody is bigger than you are. Everybody wants to be accepted. My friends thought I was strange because I wanted more math and science classes. They said African-Americans aren't good in those subjects. I don't know how true that is, but I do know that I'm good and I won the freshman science fair. My friends have begun to like me in science because I help them with their lab experiments. I rotate each week so I have a different lab partner. Another thing I learned to do so they won't call me a nerd is to crack jokes in class. I show them my grades are because of my ability and that I can be as silly as they are. So far things are great, I'm doing good in math and science. I could do better in English and history. My friends like me because I help them and they don't tease me because I'm always clowning and cracking jokes about them."

**Jerome**

Jerome attends CVS High School, previously described as

a very large school in an affluent neighborhood with mediocre student achievement. Jerome has one sister, his mother works part-time and his father paints during the day and works at the post office in the evenings. Jerome has a photographic memory, loves to read and received a double from the sixth to eighth grade. He currently is a sophomore. He ended his first year with a B+ average. Jerome describes his experiences.

"I flunked the whole first marking period. I just couldn't make the adjustment. I'm sure being one year younger was one factor, the large school was another, but the main thing was the honors classes. All my friends from elementary school were meeting a new group of 30 students each class, while with me, the honors classes had the same students together all the time. The girls in the honors classes seemed to like boys who were in regular classes, who could fight or were athletes. The boys in honors classes were not liked by any girls, and some of the boys didn't seem to like girls that swift. I think another reason why my grades were so poor was because I didn't know how to study. In elementary school, you can get good grades without studying, plus in honors there is more competition and a tighter curve. My friends were calling me a chump. One day a boy told me about the track team. I had planned to join the football team. My friend told me football players can hide behind their teammates while track men have to stand on their own. To make a long story short, I joined the track team, took only a few honors classes, and became popular with my classmates. I could not have made it under the original circumstances. I wanted to be popular more than I wanted to be smart. I also learned how to study better because track structured my time by taking away so much of my free time."

In Chapter Three, I will return to the students' experiences, analyze their behavior, and recommend strategies to defeat this silent killer. In the next chapter, we must find out why our youth associate academic achievement with being white. When did this phenomenon begin? Slavery? The integration of schools? Let's find out.

# THE PSYCHOLOGY OF BEING BLACK

"Girl, she thinks she's something, making the honor roll."
"I know, she's beginning to act like Darryl. They both think they're white, joining the National Honor Society."

I'm sure Imhotep's spirit is looking down on this conversation with disdain. It was not long ago in the continuum of four million years, that Imhotep at 2780 B.C. designed the first pyramid in Egypt. Africans went on to build 70 more in Egypt, and later sailed to America, 3,000 years before Columbus, and they built others in Mexico under the Olmec civilization. One of the seven wonders of the world, and only one of two remaining is the Pyramid of Giza, a monument that towers 48 stories, is 755 feet wide and with 2,300,000 stones, each weighing three tons each, perfectly balanced, all before Pythagoras.

I chose to draw upon the spirit of Imhotep, because many of our youth not only attribute academic achievement with acting white, but feel inferior to other students in math and science. Ironically, the first doctors, architects, engineers, and professors of these subjects were Africans. Imhotep is considered the father of medicine. Unfortunately, many schools teach our children that Hippocrates was the first. The early Greek scholars studied in Egypt at the first university, the Grand Lodge of Wa'at. They changed the names of Africans, so that Imhotep's Greek name is Aesculapius. Today in the oath taken to be a doctor, Imhotep's Greek name is still referred to because Hippocrates acknowledged where the origin of medicine began.[1]

How did this happen? How did a people go from pyramids to projects? How did a people reach a zenith of civilization, and now wallow in so much misery? Why do our youth attribute academic achievement with acting white? Why do they believe they are less qualified in math and science? Do our children know their history? What is the difference between African and Negro history? Which one is being given to our children?

There have been numerous books written to explain the dynamics of mental slavery. On a plantation or under apartheid, slavery takes the form of chattel or physical bondage. In this method, oppression is obvious and the evidence of bondage is unveiled so that everyone can see—both the oppressed and the oppressor. Mental slavery is more sophisticated, because when the chains are removed from the ankles and wrists and placed around the mind, it becomes more difficult for the oppressed to recognize the source of their plight.

In America, when the chains were taken off our bodies, what was our definition of beauty? What was our image of God? Did we still call ourselves Africans? Was there unity among the race? Did we feel inferior to the oppressor in our intellectual ability and economic development? Did we feel good about ourselves and come out of slavery with a strong sense of self-esteem? These are important questions that progressive psychologists and educators are asking, because they realize ultimate freedom will only manifest itself when we deprogram ourselves of the experience between the Middle Passage and 1865. We are going to have to confront this period, so that we can return to Kemet, the African word for Egypt, which is a Greek word.

We came out of slavery, by and large, with a European frame of reference. Many of us define beauty as light skin, long hair and blue eyes. We have envisioned Jesus in the same image. The majority of our people do not want to be Africans nor African-Americans. The lack of unity has reached deathly proportions, with the drug traffic, high crime rate, and lack respect for elders and life itself. An unacceptable percentage of our youth believe they are inferior to Caucasians in education and economics, which they probably learned from influential adults in their lives. I believe to improve our self-esteem we must confront this mental bondage that is so clearly expressed in our youth when they say, "I don't want to be on the honor roll because I don't want to be White."

One of the major repercussions of slavery was the public characterization of Africans being intellectually inferior. Obviously, you cannot enslave a people and indoctrinate them with inferiority, if they believe they're related to Imhotep, are well versed in math and science, and that God looks like them. The oppressor used all of his tools—books, psychologists, doctors, schools, and later the electronic media—to portray Africans as genetically inferior. I often wondered when Shockley and Jensen were embarrassing themselves analyzing the size of our brains to our intelligence, why the oppressor would have us raise, nurture, and intellectually stimulate their children. Frances Welsing, an African-American psychiatrist whom I respect dearly, challenged them on their premise and showed the positive relationship between larger amounts of melanin, the absorption of the sun, vitamin D production, and brain cell development.

The expectation of intellectual inferiority is one effect of slavery, and its continued psychological effect of eroding confidence in our youth to the point of attributing academic achievement to being white, is one of the major reasons for our continued underdevelopment. Jeff Howard from the EFFICACY Committee, dedicated to deprogram African-American students from this psychology, explains:

As a student takes tests under the cloud of predicted failure, and as each failure reinforces doubts about her capabilities, all intellectual competition comes to be associated with the spectre of having to admit to themselves a lack of intellectual capacity. When the expected failure is ascribed to a genetically based insufficiency, it amounts to an open suggestion to black youth to understand any failure in intellectual activity as confirmation of their genetic inferiority. Each engagement in intellectual competition, in other words, carries the weight of a test of one's own genetic endowment, and that of black people as a whole. It is the coup de grace that for individuals so characterized, intellectual failures register at the most fundamental and intimate level, one's genetic endowment and innate ability, rather than at the personally controllable level of one's effort. In the face of such a terrible prospect, many black people, and particularly black youth, recoil from any situation where the rumor of inferiority might be proven true.[2]

Logically speaking, if being smart is acting white, how do you act black? What is blackness? Being cool? In talking with youth around the country, many of them defined blackness based upon the way you talked, the type of music that you listen to, and where you went outside of school. If a student spoke standard English, listened to rock or classical

*Can a person be Black and go to a museum?*

music, and went to museums—they were White. If a student spoke Black English, listened to rap or rhythm and blues, and went to parties—they were Black.

My aunt was confused about these definitions. She was a public school teacher in Texas before and after integration. Before integration, her position with African-American students, which were her entire class, was "You will learn or you won't leave." Her students responded, many because they knew she was in their best interest, others grudgingly because they knew she would not let them leave. After integration, some of her African-American students called her "Uncle Tom" because she was not like some of the other teachers (some White and Black because expectations transcend race) who required less of them academically.

I will never forget the conversations I had with my aunt. I was in my early twenties, immersed in the Black liberation struggle, and my aunt was telling me if being Black, if avoiding being called an "Uncle Tom" is determined by her giving unearned grades, then she would have to be White. She went on to say, "I don't want to hear any of that °black stuff,' because when I was growing up, we knew we had inferior facilities, but that inspired us to work harder." I heard what my aunt said, but more about what she didn't say. My aunt was hurt that her high expectations were being classified as white. She had the same pain as many of today's students, who want to do well academically—?13?not be White. She did not want to be a crusader, and she was very disappointed that excellence was not respected by many people in the Black community, and that mediocrity was becoming the norm.

I have heard these kind of comments elsewhere. My father and I have had long conversations about what blackness is. He believed in the bootstrap theory; that if you worked hard in America, opportunities and rewards would be in abundance. Shelby Steele, in a very significant article, "On Being Black and Middle Class," had these comments to give on this complex issue:

What became clear to me is that people like myself and middle-class blacks generally are caught in a very specific double bind that keeps two equally powerful elements of our identity at odds with each other. The middle-class values by which we were raised—the work ethic, the importance of education, the value of property ownership, of respectability, of getting ahead, of stable family life, of initiative, of self-reliance, etc.—are in themselves raceless and even assimilationist. They urge us toward the entire constellation of qualities that are implied in the word individualism.

But the particular pattern of racial identification that emerged in the 60's and that still prevails today urges middle-class blacks (and all blacks) in the opposite direction. This pattern asks us to see ourselves as an embattled minority, and it urges an adversarial stance toward the mainstream, an emphasis on ethnic consciousness over individualism. It is organized around an implied separatism.

This form of racial identification presented blacks as a racial monolith, a singular people with a common experience of oppression. Differences within the race, no matter how ineradicable, had to be minimized. Class distinctions were one of the first such differences to be sacrificed, since they not only threatened racial unity, but also seemed to stand in contradiction to the principle of equality which was the announced goal of the movement.[3]

Petroni reinforces:

One of the great pressures which blacks feel, particularly black elites, is a pressure from other blacks which comes in the form of the message, "You think you're better than we are." The black elites for whom success is so important, find themselves in a difficult position. If they do "succeed," they are resented by most other blacks—if they do not, they lose prestige among other elites, their family, and their white friends.

While much lip-service is given to the rights of minorities, once these rights become a reality, members of the minority group themselves accuse their fellows who achieve success within the school setting of acting like whites. For blacks, part of this inconsistency lies in the black students' failure to substitute their *own* goals for white goals (which blacks reject as unacceptable). The black students want to be their own architects for accomplishment and change, but they have so far constructed little that begins to satisfy this wish.[4]


Steele acknowledges:

To move beyond the victim-focused black identity we must learn to make a difficult but crucial distinction: between actual victimization, which we must resist with every resource, and identification with the victim's status. Until we do this we will continue to wrestle more with ourselves than with the new opportunities which so many paid so dearly to win.[5]


Petroni raises the question again, what is blackness? Surely blackness is more than the juxtaposition of whiteness. I don't agree with Petroni that this definition should come from Black students, who I believe are a by-product of influential adults in their lives and the images—both electronic and print—that they've seen. Black leadership needs to define blackness from a positive, pro-African frame of reference. This definition of blackness should transcend a victim-loser analysis.

William Cross provides an excellent definition of blackness in a model showing stages of development.[6] The five levels are: pre-encounter, encounter, immersion-emersion, internalization, and internalization-commitment. When some youth believe being smart is being white, they are in the pre-encounter stage. This level has a European value system and frame of reference. Success and beauty are determined through White eyes. When students experience a crisis that motivates them to learn the Black experience, they are moving into the encounter stage. In Chapter One, a student named Darryl was accused of plagiarism—this racist assumption could have provoked the encounter stage for him. It can also occur when students experience or observe police brutality and view movies such as "Mandela," "Cry Freedom," and "Eyes on the Prize." The third stage is immersion, whereby students learn as much as they can about the Black experience. The fourth stage (internalization) is a resolution between being pro-Black and anti-White. The student is at peace with his or her identity and can be with Whites or Blacks, in front of the school, or in the library and lunchroom. The final stage is the commitment phase. It requires a move from theory to practice. Students who form African history clubs or volunteer in community organizations demonstrate this level. Malcolm X provides a very good example of this model:

Pre-encounter—Detroit Red/processed hair
Encounter—Prison (crisis)
Immersion—Eager to read and learn from Elijah Muhammad
Internalization—Malcolm X/African frame of reference
Internalization-Commitment—El Hajj Malik El Shabazz/ peace/committed to building institutions

As I stated in the Introduction, while I disagree with Sowell and Pendleton for comparing immigrants to slaves, I do agree that the former has been able to overcome external factors, because of their culture and value system that Steele documented. I also mentioned in the Introduction that I'm not interested in the rare exceptions to the rule that have been able to transcend oppression and do well academically, but the masses of our youth that remain under-achievers. In America, where one percent of the people own 60 percent of the wealth, I don't think we should only fault or even initially accuse the other 99 percent for being lazy. My favorite example about life in an oppressive environment is a 100-yard dash. The oppressor has a 30 yard head-start, but the oppressed wins the race. When interviewed, the winner can glorify his individual achievement and challenge other oppressed runners to work harder, or he can indict the race as Eddie Murphy did at the 1988 Academy Awards ceremony.

A whole book could be written about the role of the middle class in the Black liberation struggle and how their efforts must take a stance far different from welfare, which robs people of self-determination. (I have a problem with the term "middle class," because for many people, one missed check would remove them from this class. Income and wealth are not the same. Class status should be based on wealth, which is more stable than paychecks. The phenomenon of negative peer pressure transcends class status when it comes to academic achievement. In our student profiles, we had students from all demographics, who were not motivated by their peer group.) This book is grappling with how to restore blackness to excellence, and instill in our youth peer pressure that reinforces academic achievement.

Steele pointed out that African-Americans are viewed almost from a monolithic perspective. Remember, when I talked to youth, they too had some broad sweeping statements about what African-and European-American students do. Signithia Fordham, in an impressive article, develops this idea about how we see ourselves as a people:

> In studying the social identity and cultural frame of reference among Black Americans, I have found the anthropological concept "fictive kinship" useful. It refers to a kinship-like connection between and among persons in a society, not related by blood or marriage, who have maintained essential reciprocal social or economic relationships. Among Black Americans the connection extends beyond the social and economic, and includes a political function as well. The term conveys the idea of "brotherhood" and "sisterhood" of all Black Americans; thus, a sense of peoplehood or collective social identity. This sense is evident in the various kinship terms that Black Americans use to refer to one another, such as "brother," "sister," and "blood."

Black children learn the meaning of fictive kinship from their parents and peers while they are growing up. It appears, moreover, that they learn it early enough, and well enough, so

19

that *they even tend to associate their life chances and "success" potential with those of their peers and other members of the community*. The collective ethos of the fictive kinship system is challenged by the individual ethos of the dominant culture when the children enter school, and when the children experience the competition between the two for their loyalty. Conversely, those students who minimize their connection to the indigenous culture and assimilate into the school culture improve their chances of succeeding in school. Unlike the students who maintain their identification and affiliation with the indigenous culture, students who assimilate seek to maximize their success potential by minimizing their relationship to the Black community and to the stigma attached to "blackness."[7]

Ogbu, whom I respect a great deal, co-authored an article with Fordham which expands upon the comments above:

Subordinate minorities like black Americans develop a sense of collective identity or sense of peoplehood in opposition to the social identity of white Americans because of the way white Americans treat them in economic, political, social, and psychological domains, including white exclusion of these groups from true assimilation. The oppositional identity of the minority evolves also because they perceive and experience the treatment by whites as collective and enduring oppression. They realize and believe that, regardless of their place of origin e.g., in Africa) or residence in America, regardless of their economic status or physical appearance, they cannot expect to be treated like white Americans, their "fellow citizens."[8]

I spent a lot of time in 1988 speaking at places before or after Jesse during his presidential campaign. Students on the one hand were proud that Jesse was running. It gave them a sense of pride and expanded the possibility that the sky was the limit. America still expounds its democratic philosophy, while only White males have secured the presidency. On the other hand, African-American students told me they did not believe this country would allow a Black man to be president. I tried to encourage the students to continue to reach for the sky, but I understood which external factors were limiting their vision. The actual fruition of Harold Washington becoming mayor of a very racist city pumped the students to almost capacity.

Ogbu and Fordham continue:

> Along with the formation of an oppositional social identity, subordinate minorities also develop an oppositional cultural frame of reference which includes devices for protecting their identity and for maintaining boundaries between them and white Americans. Thus subordinate minorities regard certain forms of behavior and certain activities or events, symbols, and meanings as not appropriate for them because those behaviors, events, symbols, and meanings are characteristic of white Americans. At the same time they emphasize other forms of behavior and other events, symbols, and meanings are more appropriate for them because these are not a part of white Americans' way of life. To behave in the manner defined as falling within a white cultural frame of reference is to "act white" and is negatively sanctioned.
>
> An oppositional cultural frame of reference is applied by the minorities selectively. The target areas appear to be those traditionally defined as prerogatives of white Americans, both by white people themselves and by the minorities. These are areas in which it was long believed that only whites could perform well and in which few minorities traditionally were given the opportunity to try or were rewarded if they tried and succeeded. They are areas where criteria of performance have been established by whites and competence in performance is judged by whites or their representatives, and where rewards for performance are determined by white people according to white criteria. Academic tasks represent one such area.
>
> We also note that, since only black Americans are involved in the evaluation of group members' eligibility for membership in the fictive kinship system, they control the criteria used to judge one's worthiness for membership, and the criteria are totally group specific. That is, the determination

and control of the criteria for membership in the fictive kin-ship system are in contrast to the determination and control of the criteria for earning grades in school or promotion in the mainstream workplace by white people. Fictive kinship means a lot to black people because they regard it as the ideal by which members of the group are judged; it is also the medium through which blacks distinguish "real" from "spurious" members.[9]

This cultural frame of reference limits our growth and development. When I was in college, I chose to join the debate team. I had no high school experience and had lost in my only other debate, for high school president. In retro-spect, the decision to debate was the inception of my career as a public speaker and researcher. I thank the Lord and my parents for giving me a strong self-esteem to make this deci-sion. My African-American friends teased me for joining and gave me no support. Many of them chose to pledge in fraternities and sororities as early as the second semester of our freshman year. Previously, as Ogbu and Fordham stated, these activities were accepted, condoned and rein-forced by the powerful Black peer group. My decision to join the debate team almost ostracized me from my peer group. I was able to avoid total rejection because I was an athlete, liked to dance, and could "talk the talk." I even learned how to roller skate, because this was the most important week-end activity in local Black culture. Simultaneously, my Cau-casian teammates also looked at me as some kind of rare ex-ception and made comments like, "You're different and you're not like the rest of them." For one year I endured the pressure of living between two worlds and having to study ten hours a week just for debate. I became the best debater in the Midwest, and it improved my study habits, which is the major obstacle for any student who wants to graduate from college. In my class, there were 1,000 African-American students that entered, but four years later only 254 graduated. Many of them flunked out while pledging, roller skating, partying, talking in the cafeteria or dormitories, playing ball or records, and getting high.

This narrow definition of what African-Americans can participate in was a definite factor in the life of Debbi Thomas. Black people are "supposed" to be involved in *roller* skating, not *ice* skating. We definitely are not supposed to be involved at this high level of competition, because it requires long hours, coaching, and money. This monolithic description of African-Americans precludes such a wide array of talents to be developed. I'm sure African-Americans who had never watched the winter Olympics before were viewing this major event. Debbi Thomas had become a Jesse Jackson; both people had gone outside this "cultural frame of reference." On the one hand, the larger African-American community was hoping for victory, but on the other hand was doubting the possibility that the system would allow them an equal chance. This fear of rejection limits the possibility of success. In our house one of our slogans is, "nothing beats a failure but a try." I'm not saying my children believe it, but we certainly espouse it. More will be said about our youth having African-Americans for judges and determining the criteria for performance in the last two chapters, for teachers and the community.

I understand the difficulty our youth are experiencing when Jesse and Debbi are trying to achieve their respective goals. I am very much aware that while negative peer pressure toward academic achievement is one factor (internal), there are other factors (external) that created this dilemma. I believe it's very important to look first at where the problem started and then at who's perpetuating it. If we only blame the victim, we never get at the root cause which was stated earlier as racism and its indoctrination that African-Americans are genetically inferior. Ogbu adds another major external factor when he states:

> The lack of serious effort has developed partly because they see their future opportunities for employment limited by the

job ceiling. They compare themselves with whites whom they see as having more job opportunities for no other reason than their color. Because of their own limited future employment opportunities and the preferential treatment of whites in the job market, black students often become disillusioned about the future and doubtful about the value of schooling.

The job ceiling continues to generate ambivalent attitudes toward schooling which result in a lack of serious efforts to maximize achievement. This is one of the ways in which the job ceiling contributes to educational adaptation to their lower-caste status. The impact of the job ceiling on the black view of schooling varies by generation. The older generations of relatively uneducated parents and grandparents did not and in some places still did not, perceive the discrepancy between the job ceiling and schooling because their own occupational and educational aspirations and expectations were well within the range of opportunities available to blacks under the caste system. But if uneducated parents are satisfied with jobs available to their more educated children under the job ceiling, their children are not. The influence of formal education itself is largely responsible for this generational difference. On the one hand, they were asked to compete with whites in acquiring academic skills, and presumably in preparing themselves for similar roles in adult life, and more important, when they succeeded in achieving qualifications similar to those of whites, they were denied equal rewards in terms of occupation, wages, and the like.

The persistence of such a frustrating experience over generations led to the evolution of the belief that education does not help blacks to achieve the same degree of self-improvement as whites. Blacks came to believe that in the areas of jobs, promotions, wages, and social position in the community, they are judged not as individuals, on the basis of education and ability, but as blacks. They responded to this situation by repudiating the rhetorically and explicitly expressed educational opportunities of the schools and society. The repudiation took various forms, such as truancy, lack of serious efforts in and attitudes toward school, refusal to do classwork or assignments, delinquency, and even early withdrawal from school altogether. In other words, is it logical to expect that blacks and whites would exert the same energy and perform alike in school when the caste system, through the job ceiling, consistently underutilizes black training and ability and underrewards blacks for their education.[10]

I know a family where the son and daughter both have secured the maximum levels of degrees; the daughter a CPA in accounting and an MBA in finance, and the son a B.A. in economics and a Ph.D. in business administration. The daughter chose to work in corporate America, the son chose to work in the liberation struggle and started his own business. The father supported his daughter's decisions more than those of his son because he could not fully understand the disenchantment his son and many other African-Americans feel when it comes to their aspirations, educational accomplishment, and corporate opportunity, as previously described by Ogbu and Fordham. In the meantime, the daughter has become frustrated with her choice because the company does not provide her with the challenges commensurate with her skills, regardless of how much she is compensated.

The job ceiling is a significant factor impacting on academic achievement. The ceiling is not limited to jobs, but also to positions previously not populated with African-Americans, such as presidents, ice skaters, debaters, and people in the math and science professions. More pressure is needed on the society to expand this job ceiling, more Jesse Jacksons and Debbi Thomases are needed to expand our horizons, and more encouragement is needed for our youth to start their own businesses. More will be said about developing entrepeneurial skills in the last chapter.

Ogbu also points out:

The job ceiling does not explain why some blacks, who do not *consciously* evaluate their schooling in terms of this ceiling, still do poorly in school. Nor does it account for the inadequate performance of young black children who are not old enough to understand it.[11]

Other factors affecting tenacity in academic achievement beyond racism and the job ceiling are inferior schools and the belief that more money can be made in drugs and other modes of crime, sports, and music. The next chapter will look at those four sources of earning income. In this chapter, we must now look at the tension of being an American with black skin.

Du Bois described it well when he said we have two warring souls, one African and one American. Our students (consciously or unconsciously) want to be African and American. Psychologically, we have allowed academic achievement to be associated with being white, which for many people is synonymous with being American. The word "black" is associated by many of our youth with being cool, and as Steele noted, with being a victim. Warith Muhammad has advocated a more patriotic spirit and to take advantage of all America has to offer. While this has been a tremendous change from the teachings of his father Elijah Muhammad, who advocated a separate nation, there is a similarity. Both men were advocating excellence. Warith Muhammad noticed that African-American adults and youth do not take advantage of all the programs, scholarships, internships and other educational experiences that are available.

I am a long time advocate of reading bulletin boards. You can go on exchange programs to other colleges and countries, learn new skills, secure scholarships, hear interesting speakers and a host of other experiences by noticing the items tacked on bulletin boards. Is this considered white? Chicago offers a homework hotline assistance program for its public school students, 80 percent of whom are Black and Hispanic; yet the hotline is used 90 percent of the time by the Caucasian population in the city and suburbs. Is taking advantage of the hotline white and American? The Museum of Science and Industry is in the heart of the Black community in Chicago, and is populated more by Europeans who drove hours to take advantage of its wealth. A very good friend of mine who has a son, exposed him to museums and other cultural facilities. When the son wanted to replace his mother with a date at the museum, he was rejected because he was told he was acting white. At the present time, unfortunately, he is dating White girls.

Du Bois' description of the two warring souls is profound, because the tension is so great—holidays, especially July Fourth, illustrate it at its maximum level. Frederick Douglass expounds:

> What to the American slave is your Fourth of July? I answer, a day that reveals to him more than all other days of the year, the gross injustice and cruelty to which he is the constant victim. To him your celebration is a sham; your boasted liberty an unholy license; your national greatness, swelling vanity; your sounds of rejoicing are empty and heartless; your denunciation of tyrants, brass-fronted impudence; your shouts of liberty and equality, hollow mockery; your prayers and hymns, your sermons and thanksgivings, with all your religious parade and solemnity, are to him mere bombast, fraud, deception, impiety, and hypocrisy—a thin veil to cover up crimes which would disgrace a nation of savages. There is not a nation of the earth guilty of practices more shocking and bloody than are the people of these United States at this very hour.
>
> Go where you may, search where you will, roam through all the monarchies and despotisms of the Old World, travel through South America, search out every abuse and when you have found the last, lay your facts by the side of the everyday practices of this nation, and you will say with me that, for revolting barbarity and shameless hypocrisy, America reigns without a rival.[12]

Du Bois and Douglass remind us that we are not one self but two selves, and we are frequently reminded of the tension between the two selves when we are confronted with symbols of nationhood. This tension—brought on by America's refusal to admit its racism and then to eliminate it—causes African-Americans a great deal of ambivalence about our American identity. Take the American flag, for instance. Elementary school students are daily reminded of the American flag and what it stands for; they are told to stand and say the pledge to this flag at the beginning of each school day. As our youth become older, they become partially aware of its hypocrisy. How many of our youth are given a chance to learn and signify support of African-American symbols of nationhood like the red, black, and green flag and the song "Lift Every Voice and Sing"? Lots of our youth enjoy attending professional sports events, and the competition always starts with the singing of the national anthem. The crowd stands to sing the American anthem, and ambiguity sets in among parents and youth. What are we telling our youth by the way we ascribe to American symbols of nationhood and patriotism?

I believe blackness should be more than the absence of national symbols or non-action in response to American national symbols. African-American identity should be a positive reinforcement of meaningful, alternative values and symbols that represent those values. Our red, black, and green flag is not just tri-colored fabric; it stands for specific, important values—the red for our struggle to achieve, the black for our race, and the green for our fertile tomorrow. Our national anthem is more than a poem and a song; "Lift Every Voice and Sing" eloquently describes our saga in America, and the perspective we must remember if we are to be "true to our native land"—Africa. So I commend those schools and businesses that make visible efforts to esteem Black identity by posting the Liberation Flag and making the singing of the Black national anthem a regular part of their everyday activity. When they do so, our youth are reminded that the African element of their identity is worthwhile and special. And I recommend that Black parents address the issue of the dual identity being formed within their children—our youth want and need to understand what makes their two selves at war with each other, so they can face America equipped to deal with whatever comes their way. Have we ever had a discussion with our children about the flag? Have we ever considered displaying the red, black, and green on January 15 (King), May 19 (Malcolm X), August 17 (Garvey), and December 26-January 1 (Kwanzaa)?

African-American parents used to tell their children, "You've got to work *twice* as hard just to get your foot in the door." That statement is both depressing and realistic. Why should African-Americans have to work twice as hard? The statement confirms the existence of racism, the job ceiling, the caste system, and inferior schools. For many students who resent having to work twice as hard, they have consciously or unconsciously created another "cultural frame of reference" of activities and standards which allow African-Americans to participate with greater confidence—just as whites do, they will determine the criteria and judge the performance.

Other African-American parents have not told their children the above statement; instead, they have given their children the illusion that African-Americans are free to achieve whatever their skills and talents will allow. Words like "struggle," "liberation" and "freedom" are not part of their vocabulary. Signithia Fordham elaborates:

> I posit that ambivalence and conflict about academic effort appear to be at the center of Black students'—especially the high achievers'—responses to school and schooling. Hence, they develop complex strategies that enable them to resolve, or at least cope with, the ambivalence they experience. The strategy that seems to be used frequently by adolescents who succeed in school is the phenomenon that I describe as developing a raceless persona. Blackness...limits and inhibits vertical mobility in the larger American society. The high achievers described in this paper have learned the value of appearing to be raceless—a clear example of internalizing oppression—in their efforts to "make it." There is not much support for students who adapt this individualistic ethos, because succeeding in school is invariably associated with movement away from the community and is seen as a sign of having been co-opted by the dominant society.[13]

In our student profiles, Donna demonstrated the characteristic of being raceless. This was done at great pain and involuntarily. These students did not want to lose their blackness, they wanted to do well academically and have the option of joining a subject or social club at school. They wanted a choice of music preferences and where they went after school. The influential African-American peer group told them they were outside the cultural frame of reference, and they would have to give up their badge of blackness until they decided to act like a "blood." These rare students said no and are now raceless, tremendously skilled in significant areas, including math and science, yet they have no commitment to the liberation struggle because, like my aunt, they don't like this new definition of being black.

Earlier, it was mentioned that we need to redefine what blackness is so we can achieve excellence in every field of endeavor. This definition would have to allow individuality without being individualistic. The meaning would have to remove the victim image, so the welfare mentality could be replaced with self-determination. This does not mean we would ignore poverty, but would advocate government, racial, and individual responsibility. The definition has to allow and encourage our students to achieve academic excellence.

E. Sargent, a journalist with the *Washington Post*, describes this definition in his own life:

> While I had always been a good student, I became a better one as a result of my sense of black history. I began to notice that my public school teachers very rarely mentioned black contributions to the sciences, math, and other areas of study. They never talked about ways blacks could collectively use their education to solve the great economic and social problems facing the race.
>
> My mind was undergoing a metamorphosis that made the world change its texture. Everything became relevant because I knew blacks had made an impact on all facets of life. I felt a part of this that most blacks thought only white

people had a claim to. Knowing that there is a speculation that Beethoven was a black—a mulatto—made me enjoy classical music. "Man, why do you listen to that junk? That's white music," my friends would say. "Wrong. Beethoven was a brother." I was now bicultural, a distinction most Americans could not claim. I could switch from boogie to rock, from funk to jazz and rhythm and blues to Beethoven and Bach. I moved from thinking of myself as disadvantaged to realizing that I was actually "super-advantaged."[14]

What Sargent realized should be the goal of all our youth —youth that are skilled, confident, and are at stage five of the Blackness Model, which is commitment. In my book, *Lessons from History: A Celebration in Blackness*, that was my objective. I did not want to report history, I wanted to inspire our youth with it. I wanted it to be a personal story of our strengths and weaknesses. We must improve our options beyond the notions that being cool is black and being smart is white. We need more students like E. Sargent.

In this chapter, we have looked at numerous factors related to the psychology of being Black. But the major issue is that our youth are suffering from a slave mentality that attributes academic achievement with being white and dialetically dictates poor achievement with acting black. The key variable is that inferior performance and inferior ability are not the same thing. The problem I've been grappling with during this entire chapter is that much of the damage is so deep that it operates on the unconscious level. The victim is not aware of the problem and therefore is not motivated to seek solutions. African-American students have a difficult time explaining why good grades symbolize whiteness and being cool is acting black. They have problems describing their own inferiority, so they choose to say it's not important. I watched Frances Welsing on "The Donahue Show" unsuccessfully attempt to get Caucasians to admit their racism, or at least explain why one group would oppress another because of different levels of melanin. Many people, including myself, appeal to African-American men to spend more time with Black boys. Part of the problem is that African-American boys don't acknowledge they need a man around them, therefore when they do get together, it does not always achieve the desired outcome. If I accept Sowell's point that successful immigrants were able to overcome external factors because of their culture and history, then it becomes very difficult to implement a solution when many African-Americans say they don't want to hear any of that "black stuff." In the next chapter, we must make our youth confront their fears toward intellectual competition and bring this silent killer to the surface.

# STUDENTS:
# CONFRONT THE FEAR

This book was written for the parent, teacher, community youth worker, and the youth themselves. Since deprogramming did not happen after slavery, the objective of this chapter is to deprogram the students. The challenge is for the victim (youth) to admit deep within their psyche, that to associate academic achievement with acting white is to internalize black inferiority. In the first chapter, we provided vignettes of students; their behavior was analyzed historically and psychologically in the previous chapter. Let's review the factors for the lower and higher achieving students and create a larger composite.

### Lower Achievers

*Kathy*

—Private female high school—accused of being a show off, cute and stuck up; began to sit in the back and put forth less effort; high test scores; low grades.

*Aisha*

—Public school, middle income neighborhood—great potential, but little effort; cuts classes; takes easy courses; concerned about the relevancy of school, and the job ceiling for African-Americans.

## Lemont

—Public magnet school—high test scores, low grades; does not want to be in honors classes; afraid of being called a nerd or a fag; cuts classes, sits in the back; clowns in class; can't maintain serious effort for 40 weeks; loves women.

## Darryl

—Public school in impoverished neighborhood—emotionally affected when accused of plagiarism, due to racism and low teacher expectations; clowns, sits in the back; contemplating joining a gang.

## Michael

—Private male school—accused of being a brainiac and four eyes; tries to avoid answering questions in class; has secured protection grudgingly, by helping bullies with their school assignments.

## Doug

—Suburban public school—torn between two worlds, White and Black; students are divided outside the building, and inside the lunchroom, library, and study hall; he chooses his neighborhood friends over his academic peers.

The above students and so many more like them have ability, often test well, but are not motivated by their peer group toward academic achievement.

The various expressions of this silent killer are: cutting classes, poor attendance, sitting in the back, not asking or answering questions, taking easy courses, not studying, being called a nerd, brainiac, oreo, homosexual, or four eyes; students are not encouraged to speak well, visit museums, or participate in education experiences; they should not listen to classical or rock music, or hang around non-Black students inside or outside the school building; the students also question the relevancy of school and the future job market.

## Higher Achievers

*Kisha*

—Public school in impoverished neighborhood—strong will; a loner, and a good fighter.

*Donna*

—Suburban public school—highly ambitious, independent, frustrated over the definition of blackness; beginning to become raceless.

*Kofi*

—Private male school—helps bullies with their work, clowns in class; portrays high achievement to ability over effort to appease his friends.

*Jerome*

—Public school in middle-income neighborhood—prefers taking regular classes; became an athlete; likes female students.

Higher achievers also suffer from this silent killer—while their scores are better than those of their peers, they could be higher if many of them did not have to demonstrate loyalty to their peers. The various expressions of how higher achievers cope are: becoming an athlete, acting like a clown, not studying in public places, being independent, a good fighter, tutoring bullies, and becoming raceless. In attempting to deprogram students, I would like students to answer the following questionnaire:

# Student Questionnaire

Check one: [ ] Male   [ ] Female

1) How does a Black person act white?

2) How does a person act black?

3) What is a nerd?

4) Describe a good student.

5) What hours of the day do you study at home?

6) What is your favorite subject?

7) On which subject do you secure the best grade?

8) What is a "down" (cool) brother or sister?

9) Are you "down"? Explain.

10) Do most of your friends encourage your academic pursuits?

11) Do they encourage you in any area? If so, what?

12) Which group has the highest GPA (Grade Point Average)? African-Americans? Asian-Americans? European-Americans? Why?

13) Which group is better in the three major sports (baseball, basketball and football)? African-Americans? Asian-Americans? European-Americans? Why?

14) Would most African-Americans in high school choose to join a subject club or a social club? (Only choose one.) What about you?

15) How would you like to be remembered? As an athletic star? A brilliant student? Most popular? (Only choose one.) Why?

The questionnaire was distributed to over 300 students designed to represent the same demographics as the students profiled. The sample population included students from public high schools in low- and middle-income neighborhoods, magnet, private, and suburban schools, churches, summer camps, and a rites of passage conference for youth. Listed below is my rationale for each question and the students' overall responses.

(Please answer the questions before reading the survey results.)

1) How does a Black person act white? I wanted to better understand the association of academic achievement with being white. I was interested to see if the students would be bold enough to answer the question with this association. The survey showed someone acts white based on speaking proper English, style of dress, forms of music, acting stuck up, feeling superior, surfing, skiing, and being a poor dancer. The students had very clear descriptions of acting white, but they seldom said a person is acting white when he or she is smart. The description given of acting white, which included proper speech and attending educational activities, would stimulate higher achievement.

2) How does a person act black? By previously asking for a definition of whiteness, I wanted to determine if students would consciously give the opposite answer for blackness. The survey showed being black is being yourself, using slang, being negative and proud of your ancestors. The students were very ambiguous about blackness, demonstrated by their positive and negative answers concerning racial pride. This is an indication that African-American students need to be taught their history and culture in the elementary grades.

3) What is a nerd? I wanted to assess how commonly understood the term "nerd" was. The responses included one who studies all the time, scores in the 90's, and is unsociable. Their answers tell the major story—the majority of youth do not want to be nerds, therefore they seldom study and score in the 90's and they value their social life more than academics.

4) Describe a good student. I wanted to know if there were differences between the negative term "nerd," and the positive term "good student." The students said good students get good grades and follow the rules. One student was very clear and designated nerds as those who score 90 and above, while good students score 80 and above. I would have liked to have asked the students a follow-up question: How do you secure good grades and are you a good student?

5) What hours of the day do you study at home? Originally the question was, "How many hours do you study a day?" The average answer was three-four hours, which I thought was overstated. To be more specific, I realized I wanted them to tell me exactly when and for how long they studied. The students said they study late in the evening, and the average amount was an hour. Many students said they do not study at all. This is very significant in comparison to Asian- and European-American students. Our students do not study long enough and their studying begins too late in the day. If being a good student is based on length and quality of study, our students are in trouble.

6) What is your favorite subject?
7) On which subject do you secure the best grade?
These two questions are discussed together because I assumed there was a relationship between what a student likes and feels confident about, and good grades. The hypothesis was correct; the students said they enjoyed English and math, and they also said they received higher

grades in those subjects. It was also encouraging to read that they enjoyed English and math.

8) What is a "down" (cool) brother or sister?
9) Are you "down"? Explain.
I wanted to determine if being a nerd and being "down" were opposites, and whether any students considered themselves "down." The survey showed being "down" was being "hip," "real" and having lots of friends. The majority of students said they were "down," with the remaining answering that they were too independent to be cool with the group.

10) Do most of your friends encourage your academic pursuits? I wanted to find out if students could articulate the peer group's view of academic achievement. I was very surprised when the majority said yes, their friends encouraged academic pursuit.

11) Do they encourage you in any area? If so, what? I assumed the answer to number 10 would be no, but number 11 would spell out other, non-academic areas for which students receive support from friends. My sentiment would be they would get support for being involved in sports, music, sex, drugs and other crime. There was little consistency on these two questions. Often, students would answer affirmatively for support in academics, but when asked to name any area—which could include academics—the answers were negative. More qualitative research is needed about the extent of support the peer group provides to each student.

12) Which group has the highest GPA (Grade Point Average)? African-Americans? Asian-Americans? European-Americans? Why? I wanted to find out if students had made associations between race and academic achievement. Almost all the students chose Asian-Americans and at-

tributed their success to hard work, family support, and cultural pride. Our youth know the answers. But as demonstrated in previous responses, they choose to ignore them.

13) Which group is better in the three major sports (baseball, basketball and football)? African-Americans? Asian-Americans? European-Americans? Why?
I wanted to find out if youth had made an association between race and athletics. Almost all the students felt African-Americans were better athletes because of genetics. Many of the answers sounded similar to Jimmy the Greek and Al Campanis. Our youth attribute academic achievement to hard work, but they believe athletic ability is based on genetics—disregarding the long hours Black youth spend playing ball. I am very confident that if Black youth transferred their ball playing and study time, the achievement levels would also be reciprocal.

14) Would most African-Americans in high school choose to join a subject club or a social club? (Only choose one.) What about you? Why?
In the student profiles, it was mentioned one way of acting white was to join a subject club. I wanted to assess their views. A large majority of the students chose a social club, because they wanted to have fun. They felt a subject club was too close to being like school.

15) How would you like to be remembered? As an athletic star? A brilliant student? Most popular? (Only choose one.) Why? I wanted to measure their values and priorities. One-half of the youth chose being a brilliant student, followed by being athletic and popular. I was very pleased to read that our youth "want" to be brilliant students; it shows the desire is in the right place. I also believe they answered this question honestly, because throughout the questionnaire they were very candid.

James Coleman, in *Adolescent Society*, conducted a similar survey measuring students' views between athletic and academic ability and effort. Listed below are his findings:

Academics—
high intelligence......poor effort.....positive........
average intelligence...high effort.....negative.......
Athletics—
high ability..........high effort.....negative.......
average ability.......high effort.....positive........

Students' ranking structure of their peers was:

1. High Intelligence......Poor Effort...Good Athlete..
2. Average Intelligence...Poor Effort...Good Athlete..
3. Average Intelligence...Good Effort...Good Athlete..
4. High Intelligence......Good Effort...Good Athlete..
5. High Intelligence......Poor Effort...Poor Athlete..
6. Average Intelligence...Poor Effort...Poor Athlete..
7. Average Intelligence...Good Effort...Poor Athlete..
8. High Intelligence......Good Effort...Poor Athlete[1]..

In reviewing Coleman's first model, it becomes ironic that athletes can work to develop their talents and that's respected, but when good students do likewise, it's looked down upon. In the second model, it becomes very obvious that high intelligence and good effort are the least desired combination of the eight choices. In Coleman's model, athletics is revered, securing the top four spots. Returning to the results of my questionnaire, I believe our youth know what is correct. They know good students secure good grades because they study longer. Our youth never said intelligence was based on genetics. Many of our youth choose to ignore the solutions, either because they don't value academic achievement, or because they are afraid. I believe our youth value academics as measured in responses to the fifteenth question of my survey—they chose being a brilliant student over an athletic star. Athletics is still very important; it was second in my survey question, and it was equally important in Coleman's research. I believe our students are more aware of the limited odds of becoming a professional athlete, but more importantly they are aware of the short length of a professional sports career; and while performing, a professional athlete needs to be educated enough to communicate his thoughts to the media and manage his investments.

*Good students study.*

If our students know the solutions—if they value academic achievement—then they must be afraid of academic development and competition. Why are we afraid? Because slavery taught us we were intellectually inferior; until recently, institutional racism denied us participation in academic arenas, but encouraged us in sports and entertainment. The media reinforce the myth by providing greater coverage of athletic events than academic events. Schools give more glory for athletic achievement, and some teachers lower their expectations for African-American students, while their athletic coaches push them to the limit of their ability. The perception, real and imagined, that schools and the economy are White-controlled, has not encouraged Black youth to put forth their best effort. Our youth have decided academics is white and not important, therefore if they do not do well, it's okay because they said before they failed that it's not important. What a tremendous psyche job on themselves.

Young people, you appear very confident on the outside, but you are afraid on the inside. You give the illusion that everything is "straight up," but things are not cool and you know it. You must confront your fear. I am going to send you to the board in front of your friends. I'm going to place your name in the debate and spelling contests. I want you to represent the school in the science fair. I want you to run the hundred yard dash against an Asian- and a European-American student, and immediately afterwards take them on in a math contest. How do you feel? The game is over—no matter how you hide, you know the solutions, you have the ability, and you want to be brilliant.

All you have to do now is confront your fear. You must work just as hard in academics as you do in athletics. You must be just as confident. You must realize that from time to time you will not do well, but remember you did not win all your athletic contests. What did you do when you lost the basketball or volleyball game? Did you question your ability? Was it genetics? Did you try harder the next game? You know the answer. You tried harder and now the same must be done in academics.

The EFFICACY Committee, under Jeff Howard's direction, has some excellent models to confront your fear. Listed below are three of them.[2]

# The Psychology of Performance

There are four basic attributes of success and failure. They are ability, effort, ease of task, and luck. Ability and effort are internal, while ease of task and luck are external. When attributes are internal, they allow you to control your own destiny. When attributes are external, you are dependent on outside forces to determine your fate.

Favorite subject (math or English)

A. *Ability*—I received an A in math, because I'm good in math. I have been good in math since I was a kid.

B. *Effort*—I received an A in English, because I studied until I felt confident.

C. *Ease of task*—I received an A in math, because the teacher gave us an easy test.

D. *Luck*—I received an A in English, because I was guessing. Today is my lucky day.

The above criteria can also be used to explain failure.

A. *Ability*—I received an F in math, because I was never good in math. I don't like math.

B. *Effort*—I received an F in English, because I didn't study. I was hanging out with my friends last night.

C. *Ease of task*—I received an F in math, because the test was too hard. My teacher is too strict, he should give us easier tests.

D. *Luck*—I received an F in English, because today was not my day, maybe I'll be lucky on the next one.

In my questionnaire, two of the questions asked you to identify your favorite subject and the one on which you received the best grade. I indicated that many students chose the same subject for both questions. I strongly believe the reasons a subject is your favorite are because you're confident of your ability and you enjoy the subject. I don't think you would select a subject you're failing as your favorite subject. For example:

Favorite Subject (Math and English)

| Subject | Grade | Attribute | Future Response |
|---------|-------|-----------|-----------------|
| math | A | ability | greater confidence |
| English | A | effort | continue to study |
| math | F | effort | I will study harder for the next test |

Disliked Subject (Science or History)

| science | A | ease of task | nothing |
| history | A | luck | hoping |
| science | F | lack of ability | won't study |
| history | F | difficulty of task | hoping for an easier test |

When a person likes a subject, he normally receives good grades. He usually enjoys what he's doing. He attributes success to his ability and effort, and failure to a lack of effort. He never questions his ability; consequently, his confidence remains high. When a person dislikes a subject, he probably receives poorer grades. He lacks confidence and attributes failure to ability and difficulty of task. The problem with this approach is that future responses will not improve his grades, because he lacks confidence and won't study. The secret to improving your grades is by increasing the effort, which confident people understand.

To use this model successfully, I want you to create the following table for yourself:

| Date | Subject | Grade | Attribute | Future Response |
|------|---------|-------|-----------|-----------------|

You may want to do one for each subject. Try to avoid using external attributes such as ease of task and luck.

### The Zone of Moderate Risk
The second model is the "Zone of Moderate Risk." The

first objective is to establish goals. These should be realistic, challenging, behaviorally specific, measurable, and based on some timetable. For example, a realistic goal may be to improve your grades from one semester to the next by one letter. A challenging goal requires some degree of improvement. It should not maintain the existing performance. Oftentimes, students are not behaviorally specific on their goals. They will say they want to improve their grades, but they will not explain what procedures are necessary to achieve the goal. These issues should include number of study hours, time of study, location, study partners, and method of study. When goals are vague, such as "I want to be a better student," measuring success will be equally ambiguous. If you want to improve your grades by one letter in the next semester, the goal is realistic, challenging, and measurable. The last area mentioned is a time schedule. If the goal occurs over the period of a semester, the timetable has also been established.

The "Zone of Moderate Risk" was developed by the EFFICACY Committee. First, use ribbon or masking tape to mark off 16 feet, using one foot increments. The objective is to throw four rings, one at a time, around a peg placed at the beginning. You will determine where on this 16-foot board you will toss the four rings. There are three major areas on the board that reflect your decisions about your life. If you stand too close to the peg, you will do very well, but you won't be satisfied because it was too easy. If you stand too far away, you probably won't do well, and if you land one ring you will attribute it to luck. The Zone of Moderate Risk is between these two extremes, a place where you can achieve and feel successful.

When students take easy courses, choose to remain in the lower track classes, and don't volunteer to be on committees, they are at the lower extreme of the board. When students take all honors classes, play sports, are involved in clubs at school, and work 20 hours a week, they are at the other extreme. When Black males allow their peers to influence them to drive 90 miles an hour, take dangerous drugs, and get involved in unnecessary gang violence, they are at the other extreme. The Zone of Moderate Risk is realistic and challenging. In the game of life, where are you on the board? Are you involved in academic activities that are too easy? Are you challenging yourself? Are you overextended and influenced by your peers to do the impossible? Are you in the Zone of Moderate Risk? To be sure, ask youself, am I satisfied when I achieve a goal? Do I sometimes fail? Do the goals require that I work hard? If so, you are in the Zone of Moderate Risk.

The last model I want to share from EFFICACY is The Box. The students in the profiles had some very clear ideas about what is white and black. Oftentimes, these narrow definitions place us in a box. Listed below are various activities and possibilities. There are also two categories: one is "Not For You" and the other is "For You." Place the activities listed in the proper category as they pertain to your life. What do you see as possible in your life?

Perfect attendance

Freshman at a Black college
Playing rap music
Editor of the yearbook
Winner of the spelling contest
Gang banging
Scored 21 on the ACT and 1150 on the SAT
Joined the Biology Club
Getting high
Member of the National Honor Society
Joined the debate team
Playing basketball

Selected Most Likely to Succeed
Touring Africa and the Caribbean
Pregnant
D grade point average
Earned a scholarship

Driving a taxi
Engineer
Working at McDonald's
Computer programmer
Selling drugs
Teacher
Unemployed
On welfare
Owner of a business

| President of senior class | Dropping out of school |
|---|---|
| Most Improved Student | Suspended |
| **For You** | **Not For You** |

In the last chapter, I mentioned I chose to debate in college. I thought debate was in the box, "For You." My peers thought debate was Not for Me, and they classified this as a white activity. We limit ourselves, because we have created narrow boxes of possibilities. While historically this was due to slavery, can we use the same answer to explain why we can't debate, join the biology club, became student body president, and win a scholarship to college?

I believe the most important decision of your life will be made by you. While the next chapters are for parents, teachers, and youth workers in the community, you will make the most significant decision. I posit that the friends you "run with," will be the friends you end up with. I presuppose that if you "run" with the biology club and National Honor Society members, you'll probably become an engineer, doctor, or computer programmer. If you "run" with the people playing ball, getting high, memorizing rap records, and sitting in the back of the class clowning, you'll probably receive low grades, drop out, become an adolescent parent, be unemployed, exist on welfare, work a menial job, push drugs, and become a prison inmate. Look around at your friends, because you're going wherever they are.

*Parents and youth should always keep the doors of communication open.*

# PARENTS

In the Introduction, I mentioned this book was inspired by God and a parent in Philadelphia named Namorah who had a high achieving son whose scores were declining. Her comments provoked other parents who were equally puzzled about the peer group's tremendous influence. This chapter is designed to equip parents with information and skills that can deprogram our children from the psychology discussed in Chapter Two. The volatile period we're analyzing is adolescence, and this area in itself causes problems for many parents. As youth begin to be more assertive, less communicative with their parents, and more desirous of independence, they are also faced with negative peer pressure toward academics. Many parents have said they don't even recognize their adolescent, the change has been so drastic. The best advice I can give parents is to keep the lines of communication open, realize they will probably grow out of this period (if you don't believe it, talk to parents of grown, responsible children), and try to understand them by practicing the "put the shoe on the other foot" theory.

I believe parents could be more effective if they put themselves in their adolescent's position. I wonder if parents could weave their way through all the obstacles presented to our youth. I am amazed at the number of adults and parents who tell adolescents they would not want to be a teenager in these times. This is a very self-centered comment and does nothing for our youth. What is the objective of this comment? Do our youth have an option of being a teenager in another era? More importantly, if adults are so aware of the many pitfalls facing today's youth, does this translate into a better understanding and relationship with their offspring?

The University of Michigan confirms how much things have changed over the past thirty years. The table below reflects the five most influential factors on youth:

| 1950 | 1980 |
|------|------|
| home | home |
| school | peer |
| church | television |
| peer | school |
| television | church[1] |

The table for 1950 is filled with neighbors who spanked us when we misbehaved during our youth, and then told our parents, who spanked us again. It was a period in which 80 percent of African-Americans lived in two-parent homes. The table shows very little influence from television; that was not invented until 1948 and it took time for every household to have a television. It has always been difficult to measure church attendance; there are people who are officially on the rolls, but their attendance is sparse. The general sentiment, though, is that in earlier years if you asked ten youth how many of them go to church, the answer would be seven out of ten. If you asked the same question today it would be between three and four youth.

The most radical change among the factors indicated in the two tables has occurred with the peer group. Previously it was ranked fourth and now it resides in the number two position. This study was done nationally, covering all demographics; thus it does not necessarily apply to each family. There are some families where the table looks like this:

peer
television
home
school
church

There is a direct, positive relationship between peer pressure and age. As age increases, so does peer pressure. There is an inverse relationship between age and parental influence; as age increases, parental influence declines. This is illustrated by the following graph:[2]

## PEER PRESSURE SCALE

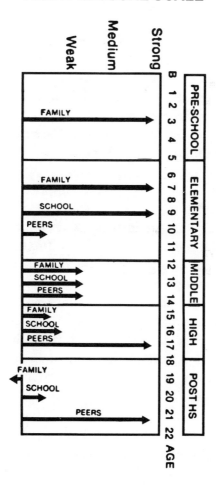

I don't know who told parents, when your children become older, they need less involvement. When I speak at pre-school programs, 80 percent of the parents are in attendance; at elementary school programs, the attendance declines to 30 percent, and the attendance at high school parent meetings in most cases doesn't even exist. Parents see the need to monitor their preschoolers' activity, to make sure they don't burn themselves or knock over objects, but they don't see the need to monitor their adolescents, who are involved in equally life-threatening situations such as crack, AIDS, pregnancy, gangs, automobile accidents, poor grades, and dropping out.

I do want parents to know, I am aware that some schools do a better job of encouraging our involvement. I am equally aware that attending a PTA meeting (involvement) is not support, which can be accomplished in numerous areas. A parent that cannot attend a meeting, but can monitor television, peer groups, homework, diet, sleep, and regular visits to the library can be more effective. Parental involvement and support are not the same. Schools need them both, but if a choice has to be made, support is more significant. I have found, though, parents that are supportive are usually equally involved.

Another major factor is reciprocal communication and availability of time. Many parents want to communicate with their youth, but it may not be reciprocal. A conversation requires both parties talking and listening. If the conversation is one-sided, with the parents asking all the questions and making all the statements, the conversation is sorely lacking. Parents cannot be totally faulted if they seek communication with an unwilling participant.

The lack of communication is also the number one problem for marriages. The major reason, beyond dishonesty, is because most people do not know how to listen. While someone else is talking, many people—rather than listening—are thinking about what they will say next. I would like parents to take a moment right now and ask themselves if they talk *at* their children or *with* them. Is the conversation one-sided, skewed toward your end? Have you ever just sat near them and asked, "How are you doing?" or, "What are you feeling?"

Communication is further complicated by parents' and their children's schedules, with parents working longer hours further from home, and high school schedules that may start as early as 5:00 a.m. and end as late as 7:00 p.m. if there is no game after school. In many households, thirty minutes may be the most time parents and adolescents have to share. I am a firm believer in having dinner together, but many parents tell me with our households more like train stations than homes, it is possible only on a few days to eat together. My response is first, is the desire there, and if so whenever possible, seek to achieve it.

The other major factor I want to raise between parent and child is the theory, "put the shoe on the other foot." In one of my earlier books, *Motivating Black Youth to Work*, I mentioned three major areas that have robbed our youth of their innocence and childhood. They were: an excessive protein diet; overexposure to sex, violence, and materialism on television; and an economy that has delayed the entrance of youth. Our children are growing too fast because of their large consumption of red meat and cow's milk. Girls are starting their menstrual cycle as early as eight years old. In high schools, oftentimes you can't distinguish the youth from the teachers. Secondly, adulthood was based on information secured through reading and experiences, but with children now watching the same television shows adults watch, they consequently think they know what we know. Neil Postman said, "there can be no childhood when there are secrets and shame."[3] Lastly, the economy has moved from the farm to the factory, and now the computer dominates. There is now less need for unskilled work, therefore society is left with youth who are overdeveloped from excessive protein, overexposed from network and cable television, and unwanted by the economy. This scenario leads to a great deal of frustration and anxiety. A sixteen-year-old male could have taken care of his expecting mistress in 1920, but he will find that very difficult to achieve today. I really don't think this society knows what to do with older teenagers. I again challenge adults, could you weave your way through all that they have to encounter?

By using the theory, "put the shoe on the other foot," it allows parents to see the world from their adolescent's eyes. So much more could be said about parenting the adolescent, but we want to specifically look at the parent-adolescent relationship as it relates to peer pressure and academic achievement. I want to give parents some concrete skills to address this silent killer. We have too many parents whose children were doing so well in the earlier grades, who now seem to have very little interest in academic achievement.

I have observed how effective parents monitor their children's peer group involvement. First, good parents know who their children's friends are. Second, they invite them over to get to know them better. Third, they monitor how long and where their youth are, and last, many parents program their youth's peer group, so that this group of friends reinforces their value system. These are just guidelines and desires; I am very much aware that parents may not, no matter how hard they try, know all their child's friends. I marvel at parents who encourage their youths to invite their friends home because it robs them of some of their privacy. It is an excellent way to learn more about your adolescent. I don't believe the gang problem belongs solely to the police. If every parent knew where their adolescent was (and not on the corner), and set a curfew at a reasonable hour, our problems could be greatly reduced.

This is not an easy task; being a father of a sixteen- and an eleven-year-old boy provides me with practical experience. In many homes, youth leave the house on a weekend in the morning and do not return until midnight. In other homes, youth attend activities that are often selected by the parents. When the youth return home from the activity, they go outside, but first they inform their parents of where they're going and with whom. Effective parents will often tell their children to check back every two hours, just to touch bases with them. I am very much aware that this kind of guideline is not foolproof, nor is it possible for everyone. My children can tell me they're going to one location with someone and end up somewhere else with someone else. I can have them check back every two hours, but it does not negate their ability within two hours to get high, have sex, and burglarize a store. My schedule simply improves my odds.

A schedule like this is not possible if you can't be there to enforce it, even though many parents can administer the schedule from a telephone. It is also difficult because our youth want to do what their friends do and will resent a schedule that is more restrictive than the one their friends have. I know it is not easy, but I strongly encourage parents to meet not only their children's friends, but their parents. Many of us now live on blocks where the children know everyone but the parents know few of their neighbors.

In that program in Philadelphia where parents individually shared their concern about their offspring being discouraged from doing well academically, I recommended that parents collectively discuss this issue. This could be difficult if you don't know your child's friends. The meeting could still be achieved by requesting assistance from the division or home room teacher. It could also be arranged by the church or a social club. The objective of this meeting is for parents to collectively share their concerns about the statement, "to be smart is to be white." Parents need to discuss how their children have arrived at this conclusion. By using the "put the shoe on the other foot" theory, parents can soul search through their own childhood and adult lives to determine how they feel about this statement. Parents cannot condemn children if they're too afraid to take tests and risks toward further advancement. Parents must ask themselves whether we too are suffering from a slave mentality that leaves us feeling intellectually inferior and with European images of beauty and God.

This first meeting, without the children, should discuss the statement, "to be smart is to be white." We must explore all the factors, previously examined in Chapter Two, including racism, slavery, inferior schools, the lack of African history, the job ceiling, fictive kinship, and a victimizing definition of blackness. When these issues are fully explored in whatever number of sessions is necessary, the next session should bring in the youth. That meeting should be an attempt to deprogram the youth of this slave mentality.

Let's review the issues. Parents are not going to be able to deprogram their youth if they too possess this slave mentality. Secondly, while this deprogramming experience can also take place at home, it is not an individual phenomenon; it took place within the peer group, therefore we must deprogram the peer group, and reinforce it with private, ongoing, individual sessions.

I believe that when chattel slavery ended, we should have all checked into the offices of Black psychologists to be deprogrammed. Unfortunately, they were not in existence in 1865, and since then, many of us have not seen the need; therefore we have individually been attempting to consciously and unconsciously determine how to be African in America. Listed below are the deprogramming questions that should be asked and answered in a collective setting. To make sure everyone participates, the questions should be answered on paper and exchanged upon completion between parent and child.

1) How do you act white?
2) How do you act black?
3) Where are your roots?
4) Describe the achievements in ancient Egypt.
5) What is the difference between Negro and African history?

6) What did Imhotep and Robeson have in common?

7) What is good hair and pretty eyes?

8) Describe Jesus Christ.

9) What are the motives for white supremacy?

10) Explain how one-third of African-Americans earn over $25,000 and another one-third earn less than $5,000.

11) Which career offers the best chance for income, stability, and growth? Sports? Crime? Education? Music? Drugs?

12) Which stage of Cross' model, from pre-encounter-to-encounter-to-immersion-to-internalization-to-commitment, do you occupy?

I cannot assume that everyone reading this book knows the answers to these questions. I also feel it's important that you know briefly my answers to the above questions. Listed below are my answers:

1) Personal opinion.

2) Personal opinion.

3) The majority of us were born in America, but our roots are in Africa. I recommend you show pictures of African people on the continent, and have an intimate dialogue to remove the Tarzan, cannibalistic image.

4) Have books available written by Josef Ben Jochannon, Cheik Anta Diop, Jacob Carruthers, myself and others that describe Imhotep, Ramses II, Akhenaten, the Pyramid of Giza, the Sphinx, and the Grand Lodge of Wa'at.

5) Negro history began in 1619, is confined to the United States, is taught primarily in February, is written from a Euro-centric perspective that glorifies contributions, names, dates, and events. African history started four million years ago, covers wherever Africans live in the world, is taught year round, is written from an Afro-centric perspective that inspires the student by reinforcing strengths and analyzing whatever mistakes were made so they can be avoided.

6) They both believed in excellence and were multi-talented. Imhotep was a doctor and architect. Robeson was a scholar,

lawyer, singer, actor, and athlete.

7) Personal opinion.

8) The Bible describes Him as the color of bronze with wooly hair. His mother is portrayed in the Shrine of the Black Madonna.

9) Possessing smaller amounts of melanin than other groups, a racial minority, and as Diop described, originating in a cold climate that reinforced a hoarding, individualistic value system.

10) The first group had supportive parents, good role models, teachers with high expectations, a positive value system, a hard work ethic, and they took advantage of opportunities. The second group did not have the above traits and circumstances, and they did not take advantage of opportunities.

11) I believe a good education provides the best chance for income, stability, and growth. The odds are seven out of a million that a basketball player will start in the NBA. The average career in the three major American professional sports is four years. Drug pushers and other criminals have the potential to earn large amounts of money, but the risk is very high. I don't know of one drug pusher who had sold drugs for forty years and retired on his surplus. Most drug pushers either begin to use what they sell or get caught. The odds are one in four that all African-American men will be incarcerated at some time. The music industry is filled with talent, but few recording labels and radio stations that will give adequate air time to unknown talent. We have hundreds of Anita Bakers, Whitney Houstons, Luther Vandrosses and Princes waiting in the wings. The education I'm advocating is not only legal, it also provides an opportunity to start your own business.

12) Personal opinion. This is a very good model for everyone. How can some parents indict their children for being in the pre-encounter stage, when they themselves are also members of that stage?

The above session may also take more than one visit. Any one of these questions could stimulate a lengthy discussion. The beauty of having our youth and parents together to deprogram ourselves is electrifying. Remember, this event can be coordinated by the division teacher, church, social club, or a group of parents hosting the event at home. The session could be made more comfortable by providing food, but I don't want anything to complicate or delay the event. This session is not going to be easy. We have a lot of years to deprogram—from 1619 to the present. It is difficult to be honest and come to grips with the idea that "to be smart is to be white." The coordination of the session should be sensitive to this reality and provide empathy in pulling out this silent killer.

In the chapter for students, the EFFICACY Program was introduced. The next session after deprogramming should use the Psychology of Performance model. Parents need to find out where their youth attribute their success and failure. The four basic attributes in the model are: ability, effort, ease of task, and luck. Remember, ability and effort are internal; ease of task and luck are external. Successful students assign success and failure to internal factors. They believe they did well because they have ability and because they worked hard. When they do not do well, they don't question their ability, they question their effort. Unsuccessful students attribute their successes and failures to external factors. Good grades are attributed to ease of task and luck, and poor grades are the result of poor ability.

In this session, ask your teenager the following questions:

1) Are you better in sports or academics?
2) Why do you do well in _____?
(sports or academics; fill in the blank according to the answer to #1)
3) What do you do when you don't do well?
4) When you don't do well in _____
(fill in the blank according to the subject area they believe is

61

their poorer area), how do you explain your failure?
5) What will you do about it in the future?

The research shows that on the average Asian-Americans outscore European- and African-Americans on the SAT. The scores are:[4]

| | |
|---|---|
| Asian-Americans | 925 |
| European-Americans | 908 |
| African-Americans | 728 |

The third session is to ask the youth to explain why Asian-Americans outscore African-Americans on the test. There are numerous factors: racism, mental slavery, inferior schools, test bias, lack of exposure to history and culture, poor parental support, and inadequate study time. The question should be asked without giving these factors. The major factors we want to analyze are: mental slavery, lack of exposure to history and culture, poor parental support, and inadequate study time. Asian-Americans also suffer from racism, inferior schools, and test bias. Incidentally, European-Americans should outscore Asian-Americans on a test designed for them and by them. In Chapter Two, we discussed in detail mental slavery perpetuated by the peer group and the lack of exposure to history and culture. The major factor we want to analyze now is study time. The following table shows the reason. Research indicates that study time per week outside of school hours among the three groups is:[5]

| | |
|---|---|
| Asian-Americans | 12 hours |
| European-Americans | 8 hours |
| African-Americans | 6 hours |

The reverse is true concerning television viewing per week per household:[6]

| African-Americans | 75 hours |
| European-Americans | 53 hours |
| Asian-Americans | unable to be measured |

I would recommend that we strongly monitor television viewing. At the minimum, for every hour of television viewed, the equivalent time in study should be achieved. So if your child watched television for two hours per day, he or she would also study a minimum of two hours. In my workshops with youth this is one of my solutions, but only when I use the word *try* do I get a favorable response. Parents, we don't know how long they will try, but we want you to monitor this effort. Intellectual performance and ability are not the same; performance is dependent on confidence and effort, while ability is innate.

The fourth session between parents and students is a role model-career expansion program. Our youth have a limited view of careers. I hear primarily, teacher, doctor, lawyer, or ball player. The first exercise is for them to name at least one occupation for each letter of the alphabet. This should generate some discussion on the difficulty and requirements to achieve each career. Ogbu and Fordham mentioned earlier that African-Americans suffer from a job ceiling. I believe it's difficult to be an engineer, if you've never seen one. This session should bring in role models to describe their professions. The group of role models can begin with the parents in the session. These role models should describe their occupational experiences and realistically portray the racism in corporate America.

Earlier, it was mentioned that some of our parents have not encouraged the mental toughness and the concept of struggle in their youth. We have youth now that are experiencing deep depression and committing suicide because they were ill-prepared for institutional racism. In most countries, students lead the revolutionary struggle, they are not content with their parents' pace for equality. This is evident throughout the continent today and in America before 1968.

The boycotts, sit-ins, and freedom rides were primarily led by students. Many of today's students are more concerned about Gucci, Adidas, and Louis Vitton than the liberation struggle. I believe that this may be the first generation of African-American youth that will not exceed their parents in academic achievement. Every other generation of our youth has exceeded their parents in academic achievement. There are parents reading this chapter who have given their teenager a telephone, television, stereo, and video recorder in their room and a car in the garage—all these youth need is a microwave oven to complete their private apartment. Many parents have given our children things, not time. The average father only spends eight minutes talking to his children, and the average mother only 30 minutes.[7] We should ask ourselves, if children receive all these things so early, what else is there when they become older? This analysis is not a middle-income phenomenon. There are many parents with meager incomes who also perform like this. I could write a book about what goes on in a shoe store between parents and their sons concerning their desire to buy $100 gym shoes. The rumor is that Black folks buy what they want and beg for what they need.

The last session, then, should discuss materialism and designer mania. The youth should be asked the following questions:

1) List the designer in order of your preference regarding gym shoes, pants, shirts, blouses, and dresses.
2) If you had a million dollars and had to spend it to benefit Black people, how would it be disbursed?
3) Design a monthly budget based on the needs of a single adult.

The objectives of this chapter have been to help parents understand the impact of peer pressure and how it can be monitored. Parents must also keep the lines of communication open. The major concern was to design collective sessions with individual opportunities to deprogram our students and ourselves from the slave experience so graphically expressed by the statement, "to be smart is to be white." We must go into the classroom and equip teachers with strategies that further deprogram our youth.

*Cooperative learning creates positive peer pressure for academic achievement.*

# TEACHERS

In this chapter, we will go beyond students and parents, and determine what teachers can do with the peer group to reinforce academic achievement. This objective cannot be achieved until we have a consensus that the peer group is one of the reasons for poorer academic achievement. On the conference circuit, I work often with Barbara Sizemore who gave me the following model:

Problem
Cause-belief
Solution
Implementation

We were talking about how many teachers want to immediately discuss the solutions first, because we are bombarded by the media and literature with the problem. In addition, most workshops will allocate 90 percent of their attention to the problem and the remainder to the other three areas. Barbara told me when she gave the solutions first, many teachers would return to her later saying, "It didn't work." Barbara shared with me the reason the solutions didn't work was either they weren't tried, or they weren't believed because there was a lack of consensus on stage two of the model.

Three of the major problems in our school system are the reading scores, the dropout rate, and the gap between White and Black achievement levels. Most people in the educational field would concur. The lack of consensus occurs on the causes for these problems. There are teachers that believe the reasons for these problems are because of family demographics, school per pupil expenditure, and innate ability. Let's discuss these factors in their respective order.

## Family Demographics

If teachers believe that scholastic problems are mainly caused by how many parents are in the home, how much money is in the home, and how many degrees parents possess, then the solutions need to be husbands, jobs, and college tuition for parents' education. Reginald Clark, in *Family Life and School Achievement*, documents that the number of parents and their income is not the major factor in developing high achieving students. The major reason is the quality of the interactions. Those parents—including single, low-income parents who dropped out of high school—that transmit hope, consistency, are complimentary, possess high expectations, and are the primary educators of their children, produce quality students.

## School Per Pupil Expenditures

If teachers believe that how much money a school allocates per child is another major cause for the problems, then the solutions need to be increased taxes or busing children to neighborhoods where there are greater allocations. Studies show that integration has not closed the gap in academic achievement. Secondly, what explains why private schools operating on a shoestring budget produce a much better product? Thirdly, Ron Edmonds conducted research of only low income schools, and he found among this group, schools that in spite of smaller allocations produced a quality product. These schools had less money but strong leadership, high expectations, greater time on task, frequent monitoring of student progress, and a learning climate that had a mission.[1] Lastly, how can Black colleges who receive less than 25 percent of the students, produce nearly 50 percent of the graduates? What is Howard University doing for African-American students that Harvard University is not doing? The answer lies in higher teacher expectations and transmitting a greater sense of self-esteem.

## Innate Ability

If teachers believe that European-American students are more gifted, especially in math and science, then the solution needs to come from God for more ability. The research shows that teacher expectations, time on task, and study time are more significant than ability in improving academic achievement. Asian-Americans did not outscore European- and African-Americans because of more ability, but because they study more. African-Americans play basketball better than other races because they practice more.

Therefore, if Barbara and I gave solutions such as high teacher expectations, greater parental support, improving students' self-esteem, a multicultural curriculum taught with a right and left brain methodology, and strategies to enhance peer pressure toward greater academic achievement, to a group of teachers that believe family demographics, school per pupil expenditures, and innate ability are the reasons for the problems—the solutions either would not work or would not be tried.

In this chapter, we will look at one of the reasons for the problems—peer pressure, its negative impact on academic achievement—from the classroom perspective.

In looking at the traditional classroom, three observations come to mind. First, the odds are 30 students to one teacher; secondly, the students lack identity, self-esteem, and motivation; and lastly, with each passing grade, content becomes more important than process, but the students don't accept this premise, they believe their peers provide a more relevant experience. In most classrooms, the teacher has one goal and the students possess another—unlike sports, where the coach and players have the same goals. Coaches spend a great degree of time instilling goals that everyone can accept. Instructors who are more concerned about content than goal setting, self-esteem, motivation, and process are faced with 30:1 odds. Unfortunately, in the upper grades and high school we have more instructors than coaches. With a national dropout rate of unacceptable figures, we don't need any more instructors.

Another consultant and good friend of mine, Habibala Saleem once shared a story with me about his class. He had spent a great deal of time instilling in the students that their mission was to improve the Black community by keeping it clean, being respectful, and working hard in school so they could provide skills to the community. One day, a student was acting undisciplined. Habibala dramatically shouted, "Who sent you here, are you an alien, we are trying to learn so that we can make our community better!" The students all turned around and the odds were 30:1, but it was not 30 students against one teacher, but 29 students and one teacher against one alien! Coach Habibala had achieved his objective.

Instructors make a terrible mistake by assuming students want to be there. In an exhaustive study done by Goodlad, it was reported students attend school because it is required, to talk with their friends, and to participate in extracurricular activities, primarily sports. Instructors believe that a good education and working hard are the avenues that will lead to success. The students believe sports, drugs, music, crime, and overall being cool is the way to succeed. Besides the fact that we have two very different value systems operating in the same class, instructors don't allow their valuable class time to be used to discuss this conflict. The objective of this chapter is to equip teachers with some strategies that can be used to infiltrate the peer group and inculcate values that we feel are necessary for their growth and development. I believe the peer group is a major reason for the academic problems experienced in the classroom. College education departments did very little for their students in preparing them to use the peer group to reinforce academic achievement.

I advocate that the first thing a coach should do is improve the odds from 30:1 to 31 people all working toward the same goal. This can only be done with a clear vision from the coach and the willingness to open the doors of communication, so that all goals can be shared. Remember, coaches will have the ability, with the information shared in previous chapters, to show the odds are better with a good education and hard work than with sports, music, drugs, crime, and being cool. I strongly recommend field trips to other places besides museums, zoos, planetariums, and art galleries. Our youth need to visit a jail or prison, criminal court, drug abuse programs, and emergency rooms at public hospitals. Our youth see drug winners, we must show them drug losers. We need to display four big posters: one for people they know that have been involved with drugs, one for the best athletes, another one for the best musicians and singers, and one for the honor roll students—all of whom are known over the last ten years. We need to place the appropriate names on the respective posters, and then review where they are today. The odds will begin to improve in your favor.

I also recommend an onslaught of role models speaking to our students. The St. Louis public schools have created an excellent role model program with over 300 professionals who have indicated an available workday, area of expertise, and the age and size of group they prefer meeting. We must show them positive role models to affect the job ceiling that often limits our youth's desire to study. I often ask youth to name five African-American athletes, musicians, and college graduates. They have no difficulty naming people in the first two areas, but they have problems recalling people with college degrees. I believe in order to be a Black engineer, you must see one. For this reason, I encourage pictures around the classroom, specifically of contemporary people in math and science. As you are aware, instructors place very little credence on room design and bulletin boards, because they are obsessed with content.

It often frightens me to notice the number of African-American students who have been steered away from challenging careers because of poor counseling. If I was principal of a school, the first area I would make changes would be in my counseling department. A society that would pay more than $20,000 to incarcerate someone, but would cut college aid and Headstart, has misplaced values that choose oppression over education. Most high schools, besides being too large, have 300-400 students per counselor and don't even offer them to the elementary grades. We need to allocate not only more money to increase the numbers, but we have to demand more from them. Many counselors are no longer in touch with today's students, and seem to feel their job description starts and ends with placing fliers on the bulletin boards outside their offices. We should tell every student if a counselor steers you away from a challenging career or does not provide the proper advice about the courses needed to achieve the qualifications to advance toward a desired profession, the whistle needs to be blown. There is no need for the oldest person in the school, waiting for retirement, being allowed to exist under the auspices of counseling.

The Black peer group can be a valuable resource for counseling departments. Older adolescents can serve as role model/counselors to their younger peers. Freshman year can be extremely difficult; it is so different from elementary school that many of our youth have a tough time surviving the first year of high school, let alone doing well academically. At the same time, their peers become increasingly important to them, so this is an effective opportunity for older peers to replace negative peer pressure with positive support and advice. Peer role model/counselors can inform freshmen about study habits and balancing academics with extracurricular activities, and they can do so from the point of view of those who have been successful with their academic experience. Everyone shares and wins in this kind of process: the younger students get some valuable information provided by those to whom they are more likely to listen, the older students feel more like an essential part of the high school they attend while gaining some important skills in communication, and the counseling staff's workload is eased so they can concentrate on doing a better job with fewer students to advise. With teamwork like this, everyone has a much better chance to succeed.

After the coach has improved the odds by entering into a dialogue on goals, the second objective would be to instill identity, self-esteem, and an appreciation of their history. Instructors have a hard time because they are trying to teach students who don't know who they are (Negro-colored-Black-Afro-American-African-American-American), don't like the way they look (good hair-bad hair, pretty eyes-ugly eyes, light skin-dark skin), and don't know if their roots began in 1619 on a plantation or four million years ago on a pyramid.

The third objective is to provide a balance between content and process. The traditonal relationship in the classroom between teacher and students is dictatorial and linear. Teachers usually lecture, but students are not allowed to ask how this is relevant to their world. Initially, students enter the classroom asking questions, but they find out with each passing year what students think is not important. There is an inverse relationship between age and asking questions. The lack of motivation did not originate with our students but with this methodology. When you train a child you give the skill first and then you show its application, relevancy, and its need. When you want to educate a child, you give the application, relevancy, and need first—then you teach the skill because the motivation to learn the skill has been established. In one of my earlier books, *Developing Positive Self-Images and Discipline in Black Children*, I indicated children know that 6 X 3 = 18, but they do very poorly determining when to use this skill in word problems. I often marvel at instructors who say African-American males don't know math, and those same males can divide drugs into fractions and sell them for the proper amount. This feat may be due to the fact that the males see the relevance on the streets, but not in the classroom.

In my book mentioned earlier, I also discussed learning styles. The brain is divided into two hemispheres. The left hemisphere is better adept at analytical skills, specifically math and science. The right hemisphere is more relational and adept at music, sports, and social skills. There are at least five ways to transmit an idea in the classroom. They are:

> written - Left
> oral  - Right
> pictures - Right
> fine arts- Right
> artifacts- Right

Instructors who are more concerned with content than process, use the written approach almost exclusively. With each passing grade, less emphasis is placed on process, less right brain activities are utilized in the classroom. Two case stories are provided.

My older son has developed more of the left side of the brain; my younger son has developed the right side more. A few years ago, the younger son had a problem with his multiplication tables. I had observed his tremendous ability to remember words from rap records. I simply converted the 8 and 9 time tables to rap, and the problem was solved. We now sell a rap tape using this approach to teach reading and phonics, called "Wordbuster."

A classroom consists of African-American and European-American students, both middle and low income. The teacher reads a story to the children and wants the students to tell the story back to her/him. The European-American students, both middle and low income, and the middle income African-American students repeat the story verbatim. The lower income African-American students add some characters and are more dramatic in their storytelling. If the teacher values rote learning and memorization exclusively, three groups pass and one fails—if the teacher also values originality, the last group also passes.

I believe schools value conformity, and as stated in Chapter Two, African-American youth have created a cultural frame of reference that is based on their criteria and is judged by them. Habibala shared this interesting number game to reflect how schools represent conformity:

1) Choose a whole number between 1 and 10.

2) Multiply this number by 2.

3) Add 24 to this number.

4) Divide this number by 2.

5) Subtract this number by the number you originally chose.

6) The end result, no matter what number you chose, is 12!

(Go ahead, try another number—you will again end up with the number 12.)

Our peer group has decided this game is acting white. They don't like the rules, it does not allow individuality, they don't believe they can win for all the reasons previously stated, and they have decided to create their own game called "being black." The game is not based on excellence and hard work, not grounded in African history, is monolithic, victim oriented, and very "cool."

Let's narrow in on the title of this book, *To be Popular or Smart: The Black Peer Group*. How can we make academic achievement popular? I have often wondered why schools give more glory to their athletes than their scholars. Where are the pep rallies and trophies for the honor roll students? I understand why the NBA and CBS give more glory to the athletes, but why schools? James Coleman, in *Adolescent*

*Society*, offered these comments:

> The activities that are rewarded are those for which there is strong competition—the activities in which everyone with some relevant ability will compete. In such activities, the persons who achieve most should be those with the most potential ability. In contrast, the unrewarded activities, those who have the most ability, may not be motivated to compete, consequently, the persons who achieve the most will be persons of lesser ability. Thus, in academic achievement where such achievement brings few social rewards, those who are motivated to "go out" for scholarly achievement will be few. The high performers, those who receive good grades, will not be those with the greatest ability, but will be a mediocre few. The intellectuals of such society, the best students, will not in fact be those with the most intellectual ability. The latter, knowing where the social rewards lie, will be off in the directions that bring social rewards.[2]

Schools must make African-American students compete in academic pursuits. Schools must give rallies, trophies, letters, and medals to the participants. I believe that competition sharpens your skills as demonstrated in sports—win or lose. African-American youth have passively withdrawn and have been allowed to in academic competition. A principal of an integrated school in Evanston told me he was not going to have an all-Black basketball team and an all-White science fair, spelling bee, and debate team. He put in the necessary effort to inspire African-American students to participate in academics and White students in basketball.

I recommend a move away from the "varsity" approach to academics and implement the "intramural" approach. If competition sharpens your skills, and it does, we want everyone to compete. We don't want only five students out of 2,000 participating in the science fair, spelling bee, and debate team. In a class of 30 students, we want everyone participating. Awards should be given not to the overall winner, but based on the greatest improvement; in this way, everyone can win and develop simultaneously.

I respect sports coaches, who each week put themselves and the team on public display. They love what they do and the players respond with mutual enthusiasm. When the Chicago public schools were on strike, many athletic coaches crossed the picket lines and practiced with their athletes. When I asked them why they crossed the line, they said, "I don't want my athletes to get behind." Where were the academic coaches with this same attitude? I'm in favor of teachers creating academic competition within and outside of the school. The Michigan League of Academic Games, founded in 1973, is an attempt to stimulate learning through constructive competition. The youth form teams within their schools and represent them in tournament play. The games consist of arithmetic, algebra, equations, set theory, grammar, sentence structure, and logic. Schools from across the state compete on Saturdays and the youth have responded with tremendous enthusiasm.

The most important strategy I can offer to teachers to achieve our objective is to remove tracking from the classroom and replace it with cooperative learning. Cooperation is one of the most important human activities. People who can organize as a group to accomplish a common end are likely to be successful in business, sports, the military, or in virtually any endeavor. In fact, one of the few areas of human activity in which cooperation is not a primary focus is in the schools.

Goodlad, in the book *A Place Called School*, found that tracking does not close the gap in academic achievement, but widens it further. He reported:

> Students in high track classes reported the highest level of peer esteem and the lowest levels of disruption and hostility among their classmates. Students in low track classes agreed the most strongly that other students were unfriendly to them. They also reported the lowest levels of peer esteem and the highest levels of discord in their classes.[3]

I have observed that schools place their better teachers in

the highest track. I applaud the Rochester public schools for recognizing that the better teachers need to be with the students who need the most assistance. In many schools, the experienced master teachers work in the highest track and the newcomers work in the lowest track. This is ironic in a profession trying to attract people and avoid burnout.

In many schools I've observed, they use the "Jackie Robinson" approach to placing African-American students in advanced placement and honors classes. They place one or two Black students in a class of all White students with an older White teacher. Do you know what it is like being the only African-American student? Do you know what it is like when Black issues such as slavery are discussed and the insensitive White teacher asks this only African-American student for an analysis? Do you know what it is like when your Black peer group calls you White, while simultaneously your White classmates and teacher say they like you because you're "different"? These are just some of the experiences encountered under tracking. A staff member in the Evanston school district told me when they increased the number of African-American students beyond one or two to 25 percent and greater, and added more Black staff to these classes, they increased the stability for these students.

My major position is not to patch up a system that does not work. Tracking does not close the gap, it widens it. Tracking is not good for integration, it is good for segregation and elitism. Many schools are integrated on the outside and on paper, but in the classroom, the lowest track is predominately Black, the middle track is integrated, and the upper track is predominately White. The psychological effect this has on a student's self-esteem, and how the African-American peer group has associated academic achievement with being white, is not worth whatever benefits—still undocumented—that may result from tracking. What is further amazing, is that the Black peer group associates academic achievement with being white, even when there are no White students in the school!

My major recommendation is cooperative learning groups. Robert Slavin in *Cooperative Learning* describes the typical classroom:

> The teacher asks Billy to spell "chief." C-H-E-E-F, he spells. The teacher says, "No. Can anyone help Billy?" Ten hands shoot up, and the teacher chooses Sam, who spells the word correctly.
>
> Does Billy interpret Sam's answer as "help"? Of course not. He is embarrassed by his mistake, and quite possibly angry at Sam for making him look dumb. Sam experiences a momentary feeling of superiority over Billy, which reinforces a pecking order with the most able students at the top and the least able at the bottom. Sam and Billy are unlikely to help each other study their spelling; they are likely to try to discourage each other from studying too hard by expressing a norm that homework is for sissies.
>
> Imagine that the structure of this classroom has been changed. Billy and Sam have been asked to work together. Now their goal is to see how many points the two boys can earn together when they take their spelling tests. In this situation, Sam will want to make sure not only that he knows his own spelling words, but also that Billy knows his. Billy will feel the same responsibility for Sam's learning. Sam and Billy want to help each other study and will encourage continued effort.[4]

The major concerns, valid and invalid, are higher achieving students will not benefit from cooperative learning, there will be chaos in the class, the lower achieving students will not do any work, it may exclude other forms of instruction, and the adjustment period negates any benefits. The best way to refute these objections is to describe cooperative learning. Johnson, et. al. provides the five teaching strategies. They are: 1) Clearly specifying the objectives for the lesson. 2) Making certain decisions about placing students in learning groups before the lesson is taught. 3) Clearly explaining the task and goal structure to the students. 4) Monitoring the effectiveness of the cooperative learning groups and intervening to provide task assistance (such as answering questions and teaching task skills) or to increase students' interpersonal and group skills. 5) Evaluating the students' achievement and helping students discuss how well they collaborated with each other.

## What is the Difference

| Cooperative Learning Groups | Traditional Learning Groups |
| --- | --- |
| Positive interdependence | No interdependence |
| Individual accountability | No individual accountability |
| Heterogeneous | Homogeneous |
| Shared leadership | One appointed leader |
| Shared responsibility for each other | Responsibility only for self |
| Task and maintenance emphasized | Only task emphasized |
| Social skills directly taught | Social skills assumed and ignored |
| Teacher observes and intervenes | Teacher ignores group functioning |
| Groups process their effectiveness | No group processing |

Johnson and Johnson along with their colleagues identified the following features that contributed to the effectiveness of cooperative learning:

1) On most tasks such as concept attainment, verbal problem, categorization, spatial problem solving, retention and memory and motor learning, cooperative efforts are usually more effective in promoting achievement.

2) The discussion process promotes the discovery and development of higher quality cognitive strategies for learning than does the individual reasoning found in other learning situations.

3) Involved participation inevitably produces conflicts among ideas, opinions, and conclusions of group members. When managed skillfully, such controversies promote in-

creased motivation, high achievement, and greater depths of understanding.

4) There tends to be considerable peer regulation, feedback, support and encouragement of learning.

5) The exchange of ideas from high, medium, and low achievement levels and different ethnic backgrounds enriches their learning experiences. Cooperative learning groups seem to be nourished by heterogeneity among group members.

6) The liking students develop for each other when they work collaboratively tends to increase their motivation to learn and to encourage each other to achieve.[5]

Two methods of cooperative learning are the Jigsaw and Team Assisted Individualization. In the Jigsaw method, students are assigned to six-member teams to work on academic material broken down into five sections. For example, a biography might be divided into early life, first accomplishments, major setbacks, later life, and impact on history. Each team member reads his or her unique section, except for two students who share a section. Next the members of different teams who have studied the same sections meet in "expert" groups to discuss their sections. Then the students return to their teams and take turns teaching their teammates about their sections. Since the only way students can learn other sections' material is to listen carefully to their teammates, they are motivated to show support and interest in one another's work. Then students take individual quizzes which result in both an individual and a team score.

In Team Assisted Individualization, each team of five players consists of students of different ability groups. Upon completion of learning the material either in cooperative groups, lecture, or individual task work, the students enter tournament competition. Five tables are placed in the room. The students represent their teams at the tournament table and earn points. Flexibility exists with regard to how the students will be assigned to the respective tables. I prefer letting the teams decide how they want to develop their "lineup" or "relay." The students encourage each other because each student is needed to do well for the team to win.[6]

Cooperative learning has been quite effective in increasing student achievement. There have been two field experimental studies comparing cooperative learning methods to traditional learning groups for eight to 16 weeks. Twenty-one found significantly greater achievement in the cooperative method groups than in the control groups, ten found no difference, and one found a slight advantage for the control group. The grade levels of these studies varied from three to 12, subject areas varied from mathematics to language arts to social studies to reading, and settings from urban to suburban to rural.[7] In another group of studies, 38 settings were created, and 33 favored cooperative learning while five saw no significant difference.[8]

Cooperative learning can profoundly affect students, because one student's success in the traditional classroom makes it more difficult for others to succeed (by raising the curve). Working hard on academic tasks can cause a student to be labeled a nerd or a teacher's pet. For this reason, students often impose norms that discourage academic work. In contrast, when students are working together on a common goal, academic work becomes a valued activity. Just as hard work in sports is valued by peers because a team member's success brings credit to the team, so academic work is valued by peers in cooperative learning classes. In this method, the higher and lower achieving students encourage each other, students translate a teacher's lecture into their frame of reference, and it reduces discipline problems. Teachers spend less time saying, "Do your own work, don't talk to your neighbor, and don't help." The students learn communication and leadership skills, group decision making and conflict management. I feel the major benefit is that in the traditional class, students hope for each other's failure; in the class learning cooperatively, students help each other succeed. This book was written to stop the silent killer, and cooperative learning can be one way to do that.

I am not recommending the cooperative method at the exclusion of lecturing and individual assignment—it is simply another method that has significant benefits, particularly the incorporation of positive peer pressure on academic achievement. The objective of this chapter was to improve the odds from 30:1 to 31 people working together. If you believe we can make a difference and that family demographics, school per pupil expenditures, and innate ability are not the issues, then you will be motivated to use these strategies to infiltrate and inculcate our values into the peer group. The last chapter reaches beyond students, parents, and teachers, and looks at the responsibility the community has to deprogram our students.

*Community programs must reward and glorify scholarship.*

# COMMUNITY

What role does the larger community play in redirecting the peer group? What people make up the community? Does the community know that a major reason for poor academic achievement among African-American youth is because they attribute being smart to being white?

The word "community" means more than a geographical area, it also includes men and women who may or may not be teachers and parents, that belong to churches, civil rights organizations, educational and recreation organizations, fraternities and sororities, block clubs, etc. I don't believe the community fully understands that our youth associate good grades with being white. How could they, when oftentimes the parents don't know. Our youth appear very confident on the outside, but are scared to death on the inside when engaging in intellectual activities. They walk around with an attitude of "no problem, everything is cool." They possess million dollar dreams with five dollar skills.

Community cannot be discussed without mentioning gangs. These groups now consist of both males and females. In past times, youth usually grew out of gangs and into a productive, meaningful life, but with an economy that has less need for Black labor, members are staying in gangs longer than before. Gangs now have members who are in their twenties, thirties, and forties. Gangs and drugs have become almost synonymous. Jeff Fort, a leading gang member in Chicago, once told me, "We will always have the youth, because we make them feel important." I will never forget that statement. Here was a gang banger with an analysis that should have come from a Black psychologist. In the parent chapter, I mentioned that our youth have experienced a terrible trick of diet, media, and economy that delayed their entrance into adulthood. This has resulted in a society that doesn't know what to do with our youth. How can the community—not gangs—make our youth feel important? How can the community deprogram our youth from believing being white is being smart?

Over the past decade, I've been involved in rites of passage programs that attempt to create skill levels commensurate with age and maturity levels. When the males and females demonstrate levels of mastery, a very moving ceremony is held in their behalf, as they are honored with being called a man or woman. In Africa, youth were very clear on this transition from childhood to adulthood, but today our youth often believe smoking, drinking, sexual activity, community crimes, and going to jail are the rites of passage.

We need to have more men spending time with our youth. Gangs are another reflection of a community with a shortage of responsible Black men. When was the last time you heard of men organized to stop gang violence or some similar cause? African-American women stand up faster than African-American men when addressing the problems of gangs, drugs, rape, and better housing conditions in the projects. The Fruit of Islam (F.O.I.) becomes a shining example of what Black men can do when organized and committed to God and the race.

A rites of passage program is an excellent opportunity for African-American adults to work with youth. My first desire, before making them feel important and going through the rites of passage, is for African-American men to speak to Black boys when they see them. How can you work with someone who either you are afraid to speak to, embarrassed of, or don't care about? One of the major reasons why our male youth especially associate academic achievement with being white or feminine, is because they don't see enough African-American men accomplished in this field. You can almost divide Black men into three groups: those men who are victims of the "Conspiracy" and have very little to offer, those men who are so busy making money they have no time and interest to spend in the community, and those few remaining men who are not victims, are highly accomplished in their own right, and are committed to speaking and working with African-American youth.

African-American women volunteer much more than men—is it because they have more time? The answer is no, most women work outside the home, work more inside the home, spend more time with the children, but still find the time to volunteer in community activities. You can now find women running Cub and Boy Scout programs, not because they want to, but because they want their sons involved in constructive activities.

In the chapter, "The Psychology of Being Black," I mentioned you cannot expect the victim to know what the remedy is and seek it out. White supremacists are not looking for Frances Welsing to explain to them that racism is a result of their own insecurities, African-Americans are not reading their history to deprogram themselves from mental slavery, and Black boys are not running to Black men because the theory says they're victims without Black men's presence in their lives. Unfortunately, African-American males are running to gangs that make them feel important and are using and selling drugs to give them what the economy does not. I have observed meetings between African-American men and male youth. The youth often don't want to be there, but they were forced to attend by their parents. Many of the men have an air about themselves that makes it clear they believe they've given up their valuable time because the theory says Black boys need Black men. They expect the boys to run to them and shower them with respect. This meeting is a rude awakening to their egos, as these cool young brothers make these men feel invisible. I offer the theory again called, "put the shoe on the other foot"—if men just remembered how they felt at 14 meeting with adults on a Saturday morning, the program could be a lot more successful.

I believe that we have to design and market our programs in ways that will make them more enjoyable. I do accept the finding that no matter how much effort is placed in an endeavor like this, it can never compete against hanging out on the corner, in the shopping mall, playing basketball, and watching videos while eating pizza. Many programs for youth take the same style as the classroom, with adults doing the talking and youth supposedly listening. Every effort should be made to make the learning experience a hands on experience. African history can be taught through a game show or via drama, rather than a book or a lecture. Allowing youth to have officers and chair part of the meeting will allow them to feel important. Many successful programs provide a mixture of academics and athletic experiences. Unfortunately, many good programs go underutilized because the administrators placed more time in designing the program than its promotion. Many program supervisors have a perspective that their activities are so good, the community will automatically respond. Companies that sell products don't make that same mistake. My publishing company will not make that error with this book. I put too much time into writing it, and a lot of money was spent in its production to merely hope that the book will be bought. I believe at the very minimum that the amount used to produce a book should also be allocated to marketing it; if not, then it should not be published. The same formula should apply to programs—some of the best kept secrets in the Black community are the programs our children need.

I have noticed that as the age increases, the programs decrease. I also have witnessed that when youth become older, especially males, they are allowed by their parents to determine what programs they will attend. The programs that we need to deprogram our youth will require that parents make it mandatory for their youth to participate. If youth are given an option of hanging out in areas previously described or attending a rites of passage, cultural or educational program—which one do you think they will choose? Oftentimes, the programs for older youth decline because they lack parental support. The other reason of course is because this age group provides a greater challenge that primarily only gangs seem willing to hurdle. Where are the churches, civil rights organizations, educational and recreational organizations, fraternities and sororities, block clubs, etc. that are willing to work with adolescents?

As we narrow in on our title, from the community perspective, there seem to be more programs developing the right hemisphere of the brain than the left. If we accept the premise that African-American youth have the same intellectual ability as other races, and that intellectual ability and performance are not the same, and that performance is based on effort and confidence—where are the academic programs in the African-American community? There are all kinds of sports and music programs, but where are the science, math, language arts, business, and history programs? There is not a shortage of African-American men involved with Little League baseball and basketball activities. There is a lack of intellectual stimulation in the African-American community.

It becomes very obvious why our youth associate academic achievement with being white—their community does not value academia either. We produce 86 percent of the NBA starters, because we put in more hours on the basketball court than any other race. When was the last time you saw an Asian-American play in the NBA? Do not misunderstand my point; as a former athlete, I know sports teaches discipline and can structure your time to maximize study, but anything done excessively will probably not be in your best interest. I am not advocating doing away with sports activities. I'm simply reinforcing what my good friend, Larry Hawkins—who has an excellent left and right brain program at the University of Chicago—has been stating for years. Our programs should have a balance; since we know work and competition both in athletics and academics is developmental. I want men to work with our youth on the basketball court and the chemistry lab.

On a positive note, we have some excellent programs that are providing an academic experience for our youth. I will only describe a few, but I encourage you to seek out more. My church, Trinity United Church of Christ, offers over ten programs for youth ranging from tutorial, athletics, Christian education, choral, rites of passage, and cultural awareness. The cultural program is called Sojourner Truth. The youth are taught the beauty of their history from an African perspective, career development with frequent visits from role models, and discussions of contemporary issues. The rites of passage program is named Building Black Men and Women, and it teaches a set of criteria of manhood and womanhood that if successfully mastered, will allow them to participate in a moving ceremony during Kwanzaa or Black Liberation Month, also celebrated at the church. The year culminates for our youth at Trinity with an oratorical contest and scholarships to graduates. While Trinity also participates in basketball tournaments, once a year the youth compete in their communicative and dramatic skills. In response to the job ceiling that Ogbu and Fordham addressed, the church attempts to provide youth with a vision through scholarships that opportunities do exist.

The NAACP conducts an excellent program named ACT-SO (Afro-Academic, Cultural, Technological and Scientific Olympics). The program realizes competition develops skills. Annually high school students compete locally in the sciences, performing arts, visual arts, and the humanities. Winners of these local events compete at the national convention where prizes are awarded. Competition in science includes a paper, project and presentation. Performing arts include drama, dance, oratorical, vocal, and musical. Visual arts consist of painting, photography, and sculpture. Humanities involve essays, poetry, plays and musical composition.

Upward Bound is another excellent program encouraging academic development in the African-American community. During the school year, the youth meet on Saturdays and take additional classes, learn test taking skills, listen to role models, and take educational trips, including tours to Black colleges. During the summer, the program becomes more extensive because they live in dormitories and have a rigorous academic and athletic experience.

African-American employees at AT&T have done an excellent job of working with our youth and encouraging them to become engineers. Many local chapters have created Saturday schools and provided actual lab experience. I challenge other African-American employees at large corporations to do as much as those at AT&T.

Lastly, my publishing company has just founded the African American Images Talent Center. I believe all of our youth have talents but often they go unidentified and underdeveloped. This center will diagnose children's talents and make recommendations, work on developing those talents, provide career education on areas related to talents identified, and provide a business acumen that will encourage youth to start their own businesses. From a short-term perspective, it will also offer tutorial, test taking skills, computer literacy classes, and scholarship assistance.

The media need to do a much better job of covering these and other organizations and should especially cover their major events. Every city should make sure there is at least one network television show that covers these organizations on a weekly basis and at a reasonable time slot. I commend WGN-TV in Chicago for airing the show "Know Your Heritage," produced by Don Jackson and written by Iva Carruthers. The show is a Black history game show featuring high school students. If we want our youth to value academics, I can think of no better approach than competing on television and receiving trips to Disney World in Orlando, Florida. Because the media and advertising are so influential, I strongly support the brother in Philadelphia who bought billboard space encouraging our youth to read and stay in school. The Urban League also had a media blitz about its teenage pregnancy program. Ed Gardner, the chairman of Soft Sheen, has done equally well with the "Black on Black Love" campaign designed to reduce crime. There is a reason why we buy 38 percent of the cigarettes and 39 percent of the liquor — advertising. We must begin to police our community by controlling what billboards advertise to our people.

Many communities, city governments, and school boards have begun to address the job ceiling that discourages many of our youth by creating business-school partnerships. Some schools have sought corporate help for financial resources, role models, and future employment opportunities. The Junior Achievement is a program sponsored by the business community that teaches youth business jargon and begins to channel them into considering starting their own businesses. The job ceiling for African-American youth and their parents is not imagined and is not going to be driven away with affirmative action in either the public or private sector.

We need more community residents instilling in our youth the desire to start their own businesses. Arabs and Koreans come right off the boat, speaking very little English, but making plenty of money in the Black community. We have a widening gap between the Black haves and have nots — the Black haves with skills, but no guts, work downtown for someone else, while the Black have nots with no skills, but guts, open "mom and pop" stores that last less than three years. If we could unite those with the skills and guts together, some of the $250 billion that African-Americans earned last year could have remained in the community. The community needs to study Tony Brown's "Buy Freedom" campaign and Louis Farrakhan's economic programs and provide one for themselves. Every community organization should teach our youth how and why they need to start their own businesses. There is a job ceiling in America, but there is less of a ceiling on doing for self. (I have to say less, but this country also makes it difficult for us to own our own businesses. This system condemns us for receiving welfare, but when Louis Farrakhan tries to use Black companies to manufacture his products, influential people put pressure on those companies not to deal with him.)

In this chapter, we have been looking at ways the community can inspire our youth toward academic achievement. The last area I want to discuss is financial incentives. Hunter College in New York City is working with an organization and a school, and it has guaranteed scholarships for all students involved. The state of Michigan has agreed to provide scholarships at junior colleges for anyone interested. Washington, D.C. has offered scholarships to students demonstrating academic excellence. Similar situations exist in Boston. I'm sure more of these ventures are forthcoming. In Chicago, some ministers have gone as far as paying students for getting high grades and remaining in school. Money also is placed in a bank account for their future college use. A recent National Merit winner from a Chicago high school was given a car by a prominent minister.

I strongly support the community's interest in trying to motivate our students in academics. The controversy lies in whether money is the best way to motivate. Many parents have always given money for grades and often give larger presents for graduation. Is there anything wrong when a minister gives an inner city child a car, knowing that the child's family will probably not be able? Every day, youth see drug pushers and athletes wearing fancy clothes and driving nice cars. Why can't students who perform well in academics be compensated in the mode most people respect the most — materialism?

It is difficult to sell internal values of honesty, integrity, hard work, delayed gratification, and a love for learning to a youth who watches over 50,000 commercials a year. Does that mean when in Rome, do as the Romans do? Obviously, some people say yes. These people cover a wide array of fields, the statehouse, city council, school boardrooms, the pulpit, community organizations, and the home. If we want to deprogram our youth from attributing acting smart to being white, do we do it with money? If so, if drug dealers, gangs, the NBA, and record companies offer more money, what criteria will our youth use to make choices and decisions? If the value is on money, then the more offered, the greater the response. People can be bribed to infiltrate revolutionary organizations for money. People can place money over God and their families.

No, I am not against financial incentives, unless it is done at the exclusion of what I feel are more important and long lasting *internal* values. I believe the best way to motivate Black youth to study is by instilling in them a love for God, the race, and themselves. They have a responsibility to God to develop all the talents they've been given. They have a responsibility to the race to restore our people to their traditional greatness. People should see an African and immediately think of excellence and unselfishness, not being cool. They have a responsibility to themselves, not to their peer group, to be the best. If we want to drop a few dollars and a car while we're instilling a commitment to God, the race, and themselves, I'm in full agreement.

# CONCLUSION

There are many problems facing African-American youth concerning academic achievement. Those problems include low teacher expectations, inadequate parental support, low student self-esteem, and an irrelevant curriculum taught with a methodology that does not recognize children learn in other ways besides the written approach. The relationship between school and the economy is a very close one. Motivation to study can be affected when youth see a greater return selling drugs than with a college education that may be unaffordable and may not produce a job. Our youth are aware that a White male with a high school diploma will make more than anyone of another gender and race with a college degree. White males can't indict African-American people about a lack of motivation with that kind of statistic.

Some of our problems are external, while others are internal. Parents and teachers can give greater support, and teachers can raise their expectations. Administrators can adopt new materials that are culturally relevant. Teachers can be in-serviced on pedagogy and students' learning styles. All of the above can enhance students' self-esteem. Breaking the barriers of racism—both overt and institutional—becomes more difficult. The combination of greater participation in the electoral process and starting our own businesses can reduce some of the discrimination. All of the above are problems that adults can address. We know all that we need to know to teach our children. Why we have not, is more a matter of commitment than lack of theory.

Most of the problems facing African-American youth must be addressed by adults. This book has been an attempt to look at one problem—peer pressure—perpetuated by youth themselves. Many of our youth believe working hard for good grades is acting white. They have defined being white as proper speech, good grades, and attending educational extra-curricular activities. This brainwashing began in slavery, where its rationale was steeped in genetics. After chattel slavery, the myth of intellectual inferiority was perpetuated by institutional racism, and the print and electronic media. Our youth are suffering from this slave mentality unawarely. The book provides deprogramming strategies for the student and parent. African-American youth and their parents must go back to Egypt to psychologically deal with slavery.

Dialetically speaking, if our youth have a set of criteria for white behavior, they also have a set of criteria for black behavior. If being white is working hard for good grades, proper speech, and attending outside educational activities, than being black is not studying, poor grades, using slang, and confining outside activities to only those with a social nature. The image of being black is one of a victim. Adults are needed to develop our youth to stage five of William Cross' model (pre-encounter being stage one and internalization-commitment being stage five). This will require more study from adults. The majority of our youth have been negatively influenced by their peer group's attitudes toward academic achievement. The few that are able to withstand this influence find sanctimony in being the class clown, participating in athletics, fighting, playing down study time, and accepting the accusation that they are white. They have become raceless; they know they are not White, and having been excluded from the Black race because of their choice of radio station, they have unfortunately chosen to be raceless.

Optimistically, our youth know that other races have done

well because they work at academics. Our youth know the solutions and want to be brilliant students. We must help our youth destroy this silent killer—negative peer pressure toward academic achievement. The EFFICACY Committee provides three excellent models: the Psychology of Performance, the Zone of Moderate Risk, and the Box. Along with my questions for parents and youth, these are attempts to deprogram African-American youth.

Teachers must improve their odds from 30:1 to 31 people all working on the same goal. This can be enhanced when tracking is eliminated and cooperative learning is incorporated at a much greater level. Presently, the classroom is designed for individual achievement to the detriment of collective achievement. Cooperative learning encourages all youth to participate.

The community must provide youth with the opportunity to grow in math, science, language arts, and other areas beyond sports and music. How can we fault our youth, especially the males, if the only men that work in community programs are sports and music oriented? The community must also award and compensate youth for their academic efforts. They must expand and ultimately remove the job ceiling, which stifles motivation and entices the sale of drugs. This can be done by putting pressure on government and business, but more importantly by creating Junior Business Leagues and achievement programs that will show and inspire our youth to develop their own businesses.

Namorah, and the other parents who were gathered in Philadelphia, we must make our youth confront their fears, but only after we have confronted ours.

Your brother,
Jawanza
7/21/88

P.S. Thank You again Lord, for inspiring this book.

# FOOTNOTES

## Chapter One

1. Kareem Abdul-Jabbar, *Giant Steps* (New York: Bantam Books, 1983), p. 16.

## Chapter Two

1. Jawanza Kunjufu, *Lessons from History: A Celebration in Blackness* (Chicago: African American Images, 1987), pp. 3-4.
2. Ray Hammond, "Doing What's Expected of You: The Roots and Rise of the Dropout Culture," Boston: EFFICACY Committee, 1986, p. 12.
3. Shelby Steele, "On Being Black and Middle Class," *Commentary*, January, 1988, p. 44.
4. F. A. Petroni, *Two, Four, Six, Eight, When You Gonna Integrate?* (New York: Behavioral Publications, 1971), p. 254.
5. Steele, p. 47.
6. William Cross, "Models of Psychological Nigrescence: A Literature Review," *Black Psychology*, Reginald Jones (ed.), New York: Harper and Row, 1972, pp. 84-90.
7. Signithia Fordham, "Racelessness as a Factor in Black Students' School Success: Pragmatic Strategy or Pyrrhic Victory," *Harvard Educational Review*, 58:1, February, 1988, pp. 55-7.
8. Signithia Fordham and John Ogbu, "The Burden of Acting White," *The Urban Review*, 18, p. 181.
9. *Ibid.*, pp. 182, 185.
10. John Ogbu, *Minority Education and Caste: The American System in Cross-Cultural Perspective* (New York: Academic Press, 1978), pp. 188-9, 193-5.
11. *Ibid.*, p. 196.

12. Dick Gregory, *No More Lies* (New York: Harper and Row, 1971), p. 172.

13. Fordham, pp. 60-1, 80-1.

14. E. Sargent, "Freeing Myself: Discoveries that Unshackle the Mind," *The Washington Post*, February 10, 1985, pp. D1, D4.

Chapter Three

1. James Coleman, *Adolescent Society* (Glencoe: Free Press, 1961), pp. 309-10.2. EFFICACY Committee, The Middle School Program, Arlington, Massachusetts, 1987.

Chapter Four

1. Jawanza Kunjufu, *Developing Positive Self-Images and Discipline in Black Children* (Chicago: African American Images, 1984), p. 17.

2. Jawanza Kunjufu, independent research.

3. Neil Postman, *The Disappearance of Childhood* (New York: Delacorte Press, 1982), pp. 10, 13, 14, 18.

4. Telephone interview with Educational Testing Service, College Board of New York, July 19, 1988.

5. *Chicago Defender*, August 21, 1986.

6. *Ebony Man*, October, 1986, p. 62.

7. *Message*, September, 1987, p. 14.

Chapter Five

1. Jawanza Kunjufu, *Developing Positive Self-Images and Discipline in Black Children*, pp. 87-8.

2. James Coleman, *Adolescent Society*, p. 260.

3. John Goodlad, *A Place Called School* (New York: McGraw-Hill, 1984), pp. 152-9.

4. Robert Slavin, *Cooperative Learning: Student Teams* (Washington, D.C.: National Educational Association, 1982), p. 5.

5. See: D. Johnson and R. T. Johnson, *Circles of Learning: Cooperation in the Classroom*, Edina Interaction Book Company, 1986; D. Johnson and R. T. Johnson, "The Socialization and Achievement Crisis: Are Cooperative Learning Experiences the Solution?" *Applied Social Psychology Annual 4* (Beverly Hills: Sage Publications, 1983).

6. Slavin, p. 11-3.

7. *Ibid.*, p. 19.

8. *Educational Leadership*, November 11, 1987, p. 10.

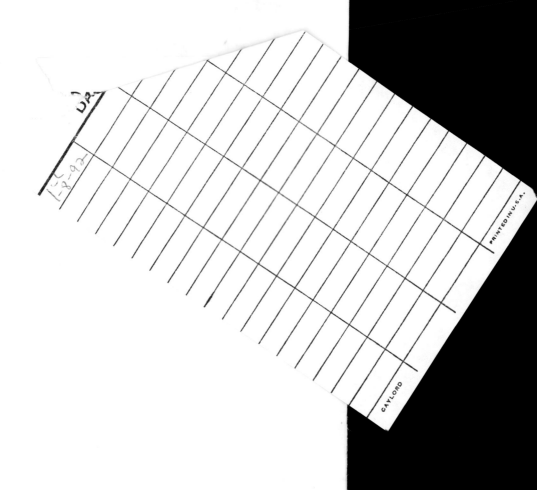